DISCOVER·NATURE

at

Sundown

DISCOVER · NATURE

at
Sundown

Things to Know and Things to Do

Elizabeth P. Lawlor

with illustrations by Pat Archer

STACKPOLE
BOOKS

Published by
STACKPOLE BOOKS
5067 Ritter Road
Mechanicsburg, PA 17055

Printed in the United States of America

Cover illustrations by Pat Archer
Cover design by Mark Olszewski and Kathleen D. Peters

First Edition

10 9 8 7 6 5 4 3 2

Library of Congress Cataloging-in-Publication Data

Lawlor, Elizabeth P.
    Discover nature at sundown : things to know and things to
do / Elizabeth P. Lawlor ; with illustrations by Pat Archer. — 1st
ed.
        p.   cm.
    Includes bibliographical references (p. 227).
    ISBN 0-8117-2527-8
    1. Nocturnal animals—Juvenile literature. 2. Night-flowering
plants—Juvenile literature. 3. Night—Juvenile literature.
4. Nature study—Juvenile literature. [1. Nocturnal animals.
2. Night-flowering plants. 3. Night. 4. Nature study.]
I. Archer, Pat, ill. II. Title.
QL755.5.L39   1995
591.5—dc20   94-36944
                                                    CIP
                                                    AC

This book is dedicated to my mother,
Edna Kelly Phelan,
who tolerated my collections, living and dead,
despite the fact that she was a city gal,
and to
Dick Archer,
who collected moths and bagged fireflies.
We appreciate his patience and encouragement.

From ghoulies and ghosties and long-leggety beasties
and things that go bump in the night,
Good Lord, deliver us.

—old Cornish prayer

CONTENTS

ACKNOWLEDGMENTS

I did not write this book by myself. I consulted many scientists who contributed their talent and expertise to the project by willingly sharing their wisdom and knowledge with me. In the course of our conversations, they clarified many points and reconciled conflicting pieces of information sometimes found in the literature. They provided me with valuable reading material in the form of abstracts, papers, and references to important research projects. Some of them took extra time to tell me about their adventures in the field. These stories provided some of the insights into the lives of nocturnal creatures that you will find in the pages of this book.

Two of the scientists who helped me are Dr. David Auth, Collection Manager in Herpetology, Florida State Museum, University of Florida; and Dr. Alfred Gardner, Curator of Mammals at the National Museum of Natural History, Washington, D.C. Also from the University of Florida are Dr. Dale Habeck, Professor of Entomology (moths); Dr. James Lloyd, Professor of Entomology (fireflies); and Dr. Thomas Walker, Professor of Entomology (grasshoppers, crickets, and katydids). Thank you all. Mrs Janet Tyburec, Education Director at Bat Conservation International, Inc., in Austin, Texas, added to the information on the lives of the bats that whir and somersault through the evening sky.

I am also very grateful to others who guided me along the way: librarians at Salisbury State University, Salisbury, Maryland; the Talbot County Library, Easton, Maryland; the Greenwich Public Library, Greenwich, Connecticut; and the National Museum of Natural History, Washington, D.C., were tireless in tracking down books, journals, and papers. They were especially efficient at unearthing resources tucked into those cryptic spaces in libraries seldom visited by most of us.

I also want to thank Stackpole Books' editors Sally Atwater and Val Gittings for their continued editorial assistance and guidance.

The list of credits would not be complete if I did not include Dr. Francis X. Lawlor, a constructive critic. Always willing to make a suggestion or two or more, he supported me through some tough moments. Thanks, Sicnarf.

INTRODUCTION

This book, the third in the Discover Nature series, is for people who want to find out about the wild things that thrive under the cloak of night. Like the first and second volumes of the series, this book is concerned with knowing and doing. It is for people who want to get close to nature. It is for the young, for students, for teachers, for parents, for retirees, for all those with a new or renewed interest in the world around us. Getting started as a naturalist requires a friendly, patient guide; this book is intended to be just that. It is intended to gently lead you to the point of knowledge and experience where various field guides will be useful to you. When you have "done" this book, I hope that you will feel in touch with the creatures of the night.

Each chapter introduces you to a common, easily found living thing that makes its living after the sun goes down. You will learn about its unique place in the web of life and the most fascinating aspects of its lifestyle. This information summarizes the major points of interest in the scientific research available on each topic. Each chapter also suggests activities—things you can do to discover for yourself what each creature looks like, where it lives, and how it survives.

In the first part of each chapter, you will find the important facts about a particular living thing, including some amazing discoveries that scientists have made. You will learn the common names of birds and animals as well as their scientific names, which are usually Latin. In the second part of each chapter, called "The World of _____," you will be guided through a series of observational and exploratory activities. This hands-on involvement with plants and animals is certainly the most important of all learning experiences. This is how you will really discover what life at night is about, something that no amount of reading can do for you.

HOW TO USE THIS BOOK

Feel free to start reading at any point in this book. If you're really interested in owls, for instance, and have a chance to observe them somewhere, read that chapter. Then read the section following this one, "What to Bring." You'll find additional specific items you'll need in the "What to Bring" section of each chapter. This section will also tell you which specific science-process skills are developed in each activity. Do take the suggestion that you keep a field notebook. You can begin this process by making notes in the spaces provided in this book.

My great hope is that this book will be only a beginning for you. I have suggested other readings, keyed to each chapter, to help you learn more than this book can provide. In a sense, when you begin your explorations, you will go beyond all books. Once you get started, Nature herself will be your guide.

WHAT TO BRING

To become fully involved in the hands-on activities suggested in this book, you'll need very little equipment. Your basic kit requires only a few essentials, starting with a field notebook. I generally use a spiral-bound, five-inch-by-seven-inch memo book. Throw in several ballpoint pens and some pencils. Since several of the explorations will involve taking some measurements, a six-inch flexible ruler or tape measure is another essential. Include a small magnifier or hand lens. Nature centers generally stock good plastic lenses that cost less than three dollars. You may want to have a bug box—a small, see-through acrylic box with a magnifier permanently set into the lid. It's handy for examining moths, spiders, and other small creatures: with it you can capture, hold, and study them without touching or harming them. A penknife and several small sandwich bags are also useful to have on hand. A flashlight will frequently be needed, and it's important to wear reflective clothing when you're around traffic.

All the basic kit contents easily fit into a medium-sized Ziploc bag, ready to carry in a backpack, a bicycle basket, or the glove compartment of a car.

Basic Kit:
field notebook
ruler
magnifier
bug box
flashlight
penknife
pens and pencils
small sandwich bags
reflective clothing where appropriate

Although not essential, a pair of binoculars adds to the joy of discovery when you are exploring while there is still sufficient light. A tape recorder will be helpful when you are listening to the various sounds of the night. A camera and lenses for taking pictures in dim light are other items you might find helpful.

You also will want a three-ringed loose-leaf notebook so that you can record, in an expanded form, the information you collect in the field. As you make notes, you'll have an opportunity to reflect on what you saw and to think through some of the questions raised during your explorations. Consult your reference books and field guides for additional information.

As you read and investigate, you will come to understand how fragile these communities of living things can be. You will inevitably encounter the effects of man's presence. I hope you will become concerned in specific, practical ways. This kind of concern is the way to make a difference for the future of the environment. We still have a long way to go.

PART I

THE STAGE

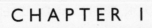

CHAPTER 1

Meet the Night

LOOK, SMELL, AND LISTEN

In rhythm with the turning earth, the sun appears to move across the sky from east to west. In late afternoon as it begins to slip below the horizon, a deep glow of reds, oranges, and yellows floods the western sky beneath a ceiling of blue.

Shafts of fading light gradually pull the darkness over the ground below and gently nudge the day aside. Night slowly fades into the spaces between branch and twig and blades of grass. Hilltops, treetops, and the sky over fields and meadows are among the last places to be filled with night. You can observe this gradual and impressive transition away from daylight if you take the time to look. Watch as day fades into night first along the floor of forest and field and slowly makes its way up into thickets and around vines, shrubs, and small trees. Watch as the darkness continues its rise to the sky. You will see the blue ceiling change from pale blue to cobalt and finally to a black dome punctuated by points of light.

Humans have been called "eye-dependent" because in the lighted world of day, we receive information primarily through sight. We see clouds scuttling across the sky—their shape and color tell us to expect either fair weather or a storm. We delight in the variety of birds that visit our backyard feeders, which we identify by their shape, color, and size. We speak of colorful wildflowers that fill the meadows and of the beautifully shaped trees that line the streets. Even at night we tend to focus our attention on what we can and cannot see.

The arrival of dusk does not acutely affect us or our lives primarily because we respond by turning on electric lights. In an artificially lighted world, we carry on our activities without any inconvenience. The effects of diminishing light are more noticeable in the wild world and are apparent even before the sun goes down. An hour or so before sunset, activity among birds, animals, and insects increases and continues through twilight. This is the time when vegetarians such as seed-eating birds grab a final snack before sleep; when hungry insectivores and carnivores awaken ready to eat; when rabbits forage for a last meal before snuggling into their dens for the night; and when the whistlelike call of the insect-eating tree frogs begins to rise from the pond. In the twilight the fragile wings of mosquitoes and other night-flying insects begin to whine. After the sun disappears below the horizon, the whippoorwill breaks its silence, beginning its monotonous call. Bats whiz about in erratic paths as they hunt for insects. Starlings, red-winged blackbirds, and other daytime birds flock to their roosts after a day of gathering seeds. Nighthawks leave their daytime roosts—in the dark they don't need the camouflage that protected them during the day. Deer, foxes, mice, and other animals that spend their day hidden move from the safety of trees and foliage to feed in open spaces under the cover of night. After their last run of the day, gray squirrels scamper up tree trunks to the safety of their nests. Opossums make their appearance, and the thrush and veery serenade the woodland. Each day in these hours of diminishing light, a drama of survival between prey and predator unfolds.

Many creatures of the night are able to see in the dark, but they are not as visually dependent as we are—they also use sounds and smells to navigate through their dim world. Many of them don't have what we think of as ears but can hear sounds beyond our range of hearing; they have developed special structures that are more sensitive than our ears. Likewise, many night creatures can detect odors that we can't smell. Some, such as moths, depend on their sense of smell for survival. Others, like owls, rely on sound to help them find meals and mates while avoiding predators.

Animals, insects, and birds signal each other in strange gestures and languages that involve odors and sounds, as well as visual cues. It is difficult for us to understand animal, insect, and bird "language" because we don't recognize the vocabulary or the grammar. We are strangers in this noisy world that is pungent with the spicy-sweet fragrance of night-blooming flowers. It is a magical world that offers us an opportunity to sharpen our senses. The night is a time to explore, not a time to fear.

THE WORLD OF NIGHT

What to Bring	Science Skills
basic kit	*observing*
local newspaper	*recording*
watch	*classifying*
tape recorder	
sense of adventure	

ACTIVITIES

Creature Survey. About an hour before sunset, the wild things that share our neighborhoods respond to the diminishing light. Animals that spend the day in field and meadow find sanctuary in the woodlands; animals of the forest leave this protected habitat to feed without the benefit of cover. Huge flocks of starlings and other birds can be seen returning to their roosting sites after a day of foraging. Birds of the open fields find sanctuary in the topmost branches of trees. Gray squirrels, too, hurry up tree trunks to spend the dark hours in the security of their nests. Opossums leave their dens to forage hidden by the underbrush, and small birds begin their evening song. You can expect to find deer, red and gray foxes, skunks, and raccoons feeding beside streams and rivulets. While the creatures of the day find rest in the dark, their nocturnal neighbors go to work.

How many of these night laborers can you find? Sometimes when you use a tape recorder, you can discover sounds that you missed. Can you figure out how they are equipped to do their jobs in the dark? The chart below will help you organize your survey of the animals and insects you find at this time of day.

Date	Animals	Insects	Birds	Comments

How Long Does It Take Dark to Come? Night does not drop on us from above like a shower from a rain cloud but rises slowly from the ground, settling in gradually over a period of hours. Darkness reaches the sky long after it has enveloped the earth. You can observe this as the sky color shifts from pale blue to cobalt blue to black. How long after the sun disappears below the horizon does it take for the sky to become black?

Time, Sunset, and Degrees. Time is said to be a measure of change. The basic change we observe every day is the shift from day to night and then from night to day. We can divide this change into twenty-four equal time periods that reflect the apparent motion of the sun across the sky.

If the earth makes one complete turn (360 degrees) on its axis in twenty-four hours, then it will turn about 15 degrees in one hour. As this happens the sun appears to move across the sky, so it is convenient for us to say that the sun moves 15 degrees every hour, or about 7.5 degrees every thirty minutes. Using this formula, we know that the sun is 15 degrees below the horizon one hour after we see it sink from view.

You can use these concepts in the activity that follows.

Twilight's Official Names. The portion of the day between dusk and dark has been conveniently divided into two periods called "civil twilight" and "nautical twilight." These represent blocks of time that are distinguished by the number of degrees that the sun is below the horizon. You will also notice changes in what you are able to see.

Civil twilight comes when the sun is no more than six degrees below the horizon. When does civil twilight occur in your neighborhood? Keep a record of when this occurs for about two weeks. What do you observe?

Nautical twilight occurs when the sun is between six and twelve degrees below the horizon. During what time will this occur in your area? How does the time of nautical twilight change over a period of time? When can you see stars? When does the horizon disappear? When does the general outline of trees grow vague?

To find out when civil twilight and nautical twilight occur in your area, you will need to know the official time of sunset (check your local newspaper). You will notice that sunset occurs at a different time each day. What do you notice about the changing time? Is there a pattern to it?

CHAPTER 2

Smells

IT'S NOT ALWAYS THE NOSE THAT KNOWS

Many night animals depend on smell more than any other sense. We don't often recognize smell for what it is—a chemical sense that, along with taste, gives living things the ability to detect chemicals in their environment. This ability can be seen in one of the most primitive life-forms still surviving today, the amoeba. That single-celled protozoan, which most of us meet in high school biology, is able to discriminate between a morsel of food and a particle of sand in the water by detecting and evaluating chemicals dissolved in the water. A small bit of food in the water releases submicroscopic bits of itself called molecules. The amoeba then detects these molecules, which lead it to the food.

Animals that live on land have a similar chemical-detection sense that picks up molecules released by many objects into the air. You experience this every time you smell the fragrance of your favorite perfume, detect the aroma of food cooking, or pick up odors that may not be so pleasant. Like other mammals, we have special detection cells in our nasal passages.

Salmon, renowned for their ability to return to the waters of their birth to spawn, have "noses," or chemoreceptors, on top of their heads. These chemical detectors may explain why the fish is able to "read" geographical cues in the water.

Insects use similar chemical tricks to find out about the world beyond their hard, protein "skin." Sensitive antennae tell them about the world far beyond their reach or vision by detecting chemical molecules that travel on air currents. The honeybee has about 30,000 tiny "pegs" on its antennae. Because these are sensitive to odors, they guide the honeybee to distant food and to special plants on which to lay its eggs. Ants similarly use their antennae to help them get around in their world. Antennae are especially large in insects with poor eyesight.

Moths have short, feathery antennae and an incredible sense of smell. Some male moths have been known to respond to the scent of a female more than a mile away. A female silkworm moth has a scent that is effective as a lure in concentrations as little as 1/80,000,000,000,000. Moths use their sense of smell almost to the exclusion of any other senses, and a male moth missing one antennae is at a significant disadvantage. Although he can detect the odor of a female of his species, he is unable to determine her precise location.

Other types of insects have chemical detectors on their legs and abdomens. Still other species have these chemical receivers in their mouths, and you can find female insects with them on their ovipositors, the organs they

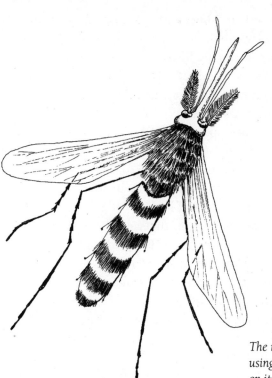

The male mosquito smells by using specialized sensory cells on its antennae.

use to lay their eggs. The taste receptors of butterflies and flies are located on the front legs, not around the mouth: they smell and taste their food by walking on it.

The flashing, forked tongue of a snake is not used to sting its enemies, as folklore tells, but it does play a vital role in providing the snake with information about its world. During its rapid flashing, the tongue takes chemical samples of air and inserts them into the two pockets located in the roof of the snake's mouth. These chemical samples may contain the odor of its prey or indicate the approach of a predator. They may tell the snake not only that you are present, but also that you are frightened.

Odor also plays an interesting role in the lives of frogs. Scientists believe that odors from oils in algae and decaying animal and vegetable matter emanate from ponds and streams in the spring. Since frogs spend the winter away from their breeding ponds, the information that the frogs learn from these odors is very important.

Birds rely primarily on vision, and most of them do not have a well-developed sense of smell; vultures are a notable exception. The large nostrils and olfactory bulbs in the brains of these birds help them locate dead and decaying animal material. Where I live in Maryland, turkey vultures make loose circles in the sky as they search for death in the fields below. The volatile by-products of decomposition are lifted by air currents that carry their message to the high-flying birds. This is an advantage to the vultures because they are competing with ground scavengers such as carrion beetles and ants that swarm in for their share of the meal.

Bats demonstrate a different response to odors. Those who have explored caves used by hibernating bats know that the ammonia from their droppings creates quite a stench. The bats seem oblivious to this smell, but they are very much aware of other, more subtle odors in their caves. In some species, males mark females with their scent, and bats use other secretions to mark their living space. These are very important strategies when thousands of them are crammed into tight spaces in dark caves. Body odor plays an important role in helping mothers identify their young amid a crowd of baby bats. Odors given off by bats are so characteristic of their particular species that many field biologists can identify the bat species living there by the smell of the cave.

Cats have a special organ in the roofs of their mouths, called the Jacobson organ, that augments their sense of smell. Human newborns have this organ, too, but it is absorbed shortly after birth. Its presence suggests that our ancestors may have had a much more acute sense of smell than we now enjoy.

Burrowing moles neither see nor hear but use their acute sense of smell to find out about their world. Reliance on the sense of smell doesn't mean the animal always has poor eyesight, however. Our good friend the dog is an example of an animal that is an Olympian smeller but has good vision as well.

Smell is a relatively simple sense, not requiring delicate bones that articulate, as hearing does, or liquids of different densities to bend light rays, as necessary for sight. Relative to our eyes and ears, the human nose is a simple device. It has two nasal cavities that are separated by a divider called the septum. The nasal cavities have two jobs. First, they serve as air filters, as each nasal passage is furnished with tiny hairs that catch and hold debris. Second, they act as heaters, warming the air as it passes up the nasal cavities. Specialized cells with tiny hairs (cilia) form the olfactory membrane at the top of the nasal cavities. Nerves leading from these ciliated cells send impulses to the olfactory bulb in the brain, where they are detected as specific smells.

The air we breathe contains nitrogen, oxygen, carbon dioxide, and other gases. It also holds dust particles and the molecules of other substances that give us clues to what is happening around us. In order for us to smell our morning coffee, coffee molecules must constantly be leaving the surface and moving with the air. As air currents swirl imperceptibly around us, the coffee molecules reach our nose and travel up the nasal cavities to the olfactory membrane. From there impulses are sent to the brain, where they are translated as the smell we call "coffee."

Scientists classify things in order to understand how the world works. For example, researchers have grouped the cells in the retina of the eye into two types of cells—cones, for color vision, and rods, for black-and-white vision. Our understanding of vision, hearing, and taste has benefited from classification, but the sense of smell is much more elusive. People have been trying to classify smells for thousands of years, but it's been difficult. For example, the Greek philosopher Plato tried to catalog different smells by calling them pleasant or unpleasant. In the middle of the eighteenth century, Linnaeus, the Swedish botanist who became a champion classifier, grouped smells into seven categories: fragrant, garliclike (alliaceous), nauseous, musky (ambrosial), goat- or cheeselike (hircine), aromatic, and repulsive.

This system was later revised by Hendrick Zwaardemaker (1857–1930), a Dutch physiologist who grouped odors according to the following groups: ethereal (fruit, beeswax), aromatic (almonds, clover, camphor), fragrant (vanilla, balsam, flowers), ambrosial (amber, musk), alliaceous (onion, garlic, iodine), empyreumatic (roasted coffee, tobacco smoke), caprylic (cheese, sweat, goats), repulsive (narcotics, nightshade), and nauseating (carrion, feces).

In 1916 Hans Henning proposed a scheme with six major groups: putrid (foul), ethereal (fruity), resinous, spicy, fragrant (floral), and burned. In his scheme each of these odors were on the points in a five-sided prism. He believed that all odors would fall somewhere among these classes. For example, cloves are closer to spicy than they are to floral, and lemon is closer to fruity than it is to resinous.

Problems with each of these models included the omission of certain smells. Also, objective analysis is difficult because people's reactions to odors vary greatly according to age, sex, and other factors. For example, preadolescents prefer the smell of strawberries, yet with sexual maturity, neither boys nor girls find this odor especially appealing: the boys favor musk whereas older girls and young women prefer lavender. The perfume industry has parlayed this knowledge into financial success of some significance.

Today the search for a more comprehensive system for classifying elusive smells continues, and some interesting models are being developed. You can experiment yourself in the activities part of this chapter.

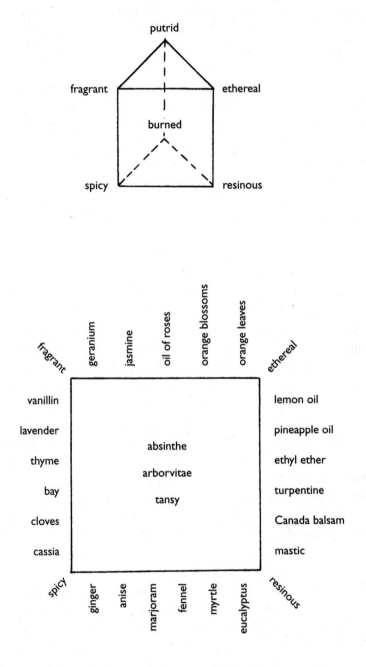

Hans Henning's scheme of odors

THE WORLD OF SMELL

What to Bring	Science Skills
basic kit	*observing*
	classifying
	comparing
	inferring

ACTIVITIES

Scientists from different specialties agree that over the years we human beings have become less dependent on our ability to discriminate odors. In our daily activities we use sight and hearing almost to the exclusion of our sense of smell. Unlike our ancestors, who had to use every sense fully in order to simply stay alive, our talent for identifying and remembering the huge number of odors that bombard our olfactory receptors has diminished. Nocturnal insects and animals, however, continue to sniff their way through the night to find food and mates—and avoid danger. The activities below are an invitation into the world of odors. Whether you find the smells redolent, pungent, fetid, or sweet, it is hoped that you will discover a new way of learning about the dark world.

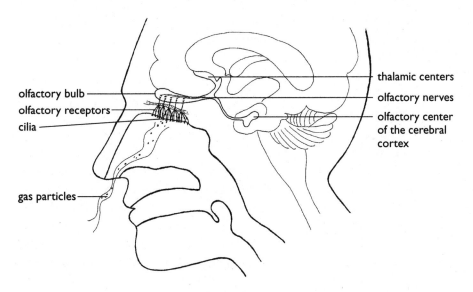

cutaway view of the nasal passages

An Olfactory Census. The night air carries many odors. Sit undisturbed for about fifteen minutes and concentrate on the smells that surround you. What specific odors can you detect? You may not be able to identify all of them. Try to compare these to familiar odors. Keep a list of them in your field notebook and be sure to indicate the weather conditions such as temperature, humidity, and wind speed and direction.

If you conduct your first census after a long, hot, dry period, do it again when it is hot and humid. What differences did you notice? (See Chapter Note 1.) Is cold weather better or worse than warm for detecting odors?

If a breeze is blowing, put your nose close to the ground. Can you pick up more odors than when you are seated? What seems to be the best height for different odors? As you repeat the activity do you notice an improvement in your skill? (Experienced hunters report that they frequently smell their prey before they see them.) Once you have sharpened your olfactory skills you can practice anywhere: in the city, in the suburbs, at the shore. Each location will reward the inquiring nose.

Comparison of Sniffers. Awareness of odors shows a wide variation among us. Perhaps if we constantly try to detect odors we will find that most people have capacities that they never dreamed of. To find out how your sense of smell compares with that of your friends, try the above activity with some friends. There is no value judgment attached to this census, but you could find out if someone you know has a future in the perfume industry. Professional perfumers are sensitive to a wide variety of odors, and they have developed a vast memory bank of blends of odors. Could this be an untapped trove of skill that we all possess?

Moisture and Smells. Hold a handful of litter such as leaves, moss, and soil and smell it. Describe the odor. How does it change if the litter is wet, as it would be after a rain? Taste and smell are closely related senses. Can you "taste" the odors?

Smells and History. Smells are often responsible for helping us reach back into our personal history. Whenever I smell burning leaves in the fall, I always think of high school football games. The memories are often pleasant, but the fragrances may also remind us of unhappy times. In your field journal keep a record of odors and past events they caused you to remember. Some of us are more successful at this than others. How is your fragrance recall? In your reading have you encountered authors who are aware of this phenomenon?

Fragrance Categories. Grouping odors according to fragrances can be

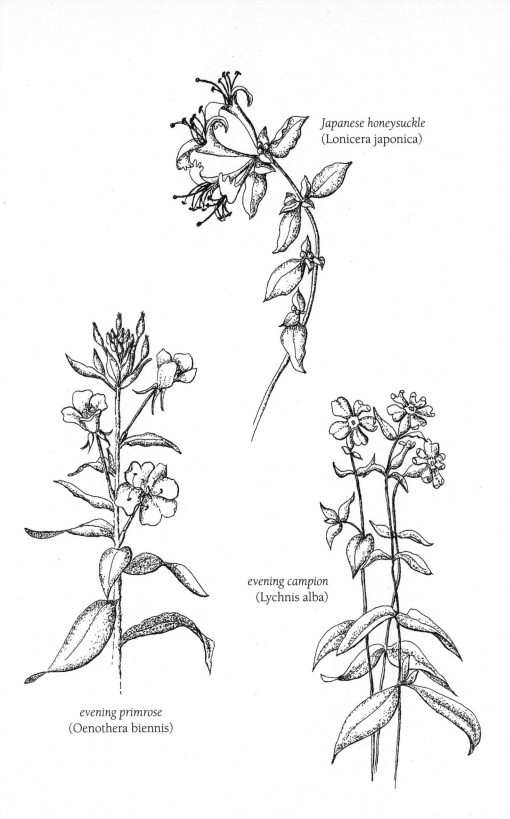

Japanese honeysuckle
(Lonicera japonica)

evening campion
(Lychnis alba)

evening primrose
(Oenothera biennis)

difficult. With the help of the descriptions of floral fragrances below, categorize the night-blooming flowers you find. Which category has the most flowers?

Lemon. These flowers contain citral, which is the chemical that gives bay leaves and the oils of lemon and orange their characteristic smells. Although not commonly found in garden flowers, you can detect its presence in magnolias, four-o'clocks, and nocturnal daylilies.

Foxy. Refers to the slightly musk odor of some night-flowering tropical plants pollinated by bats and not usually found in North America. Some wildflowers are described as foxy, or ferine, because they bring to mind the scent of wild animals.

Aromatic. This term refers to flowers that have a spicy fragrance. The scent is the result of a mix of cinnabic alcohol, eugenol, and vanilla. Heliotropes, nicotiana, spicebush (*Lindera benzoin*), and common sagebrush are examples of flowers scented by these chemicals.

Heavy. "Sweet smelling" and "overpowering" are words used to describe the flower blooms in this group, which includes mock orange (*Philadelphus* spp.), tuberoses, a few lilies, and some honeysuckles. For those that speak the language of chemistry, these scents contain benzyl acetate, indole, and methyl anthranilate.

Nose Fatigue. Cells in the olfactory center are specialized to respond to each of more than fifty basic odors. One of the things you may have noticed when continuously exposed to a particular odor is that you become "immune" to it even though you can still pick up other smells. Find out how long you can detect a particular odor before this happens. Use substances that fall into the groups established by Henning.

Night-blooming Flowers. Flowers that bloom after the sun goes down do not wear the bright, gaudy colors of their daytime sisters. Instead, their blossoms are washed in white, cream, pale yellow, or pink because the pollinators they attract are active at night. There is no need to wear flashy colors when they cannot be seen. Examples of night-blooming flowers include honeysuckle (*Lonicera* spp.), evening primrose (*Oenothera biennis*), moonflower (*Ipomoea alba*), four-o'clocks (*Mirabilis jalapa*), night-blooming catchfly (*Silene noctiflora*), dame's-rocket (*Hesperis matronalis*), and meadowsweet (*Filipendula ulmaria*). (See Chapter Note 2.)

Many night-blooming flowers thrive in the Southwest. Included in this group are such notables as angel's-trumpet (*Acleisanthes longiflora*), southwestern ringstem (*Anulocaulis leisolenus*), cottonweed (*Froelichia drummondii*),

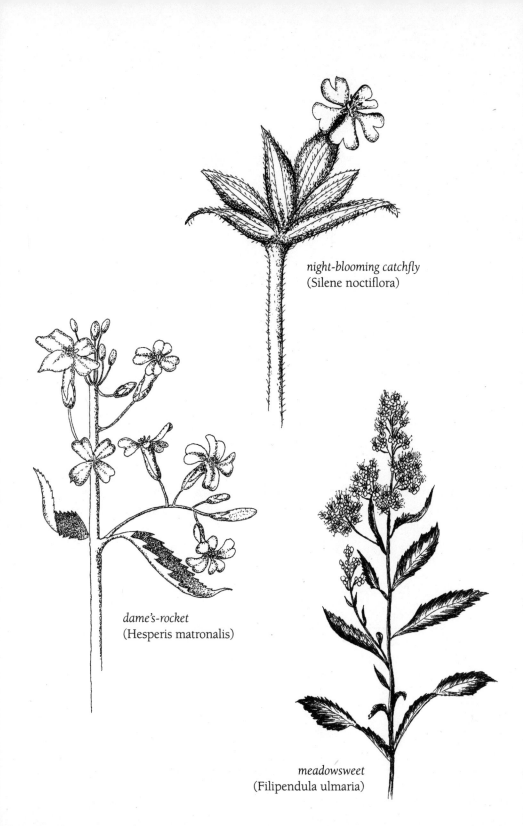

night-blooming catchfly
(Silene noctiflora)

dame's-rocket
(Hesperis matronalis)

meadowsweet
(Filipendula ulmaria)

angel's-trumpet
(Acleisanthes longiflora)

and scarlet gaura *(Gaura coccinea)*. If you live in the Southwest, look for these flowers and their pollinators.

Night Pollinators. Look for night-pollinating moths. What flowers do you find them pollinating? Does a moth specialize in a particular flower, or is it a generalist flitting from one type to another?

MOTH POLLINATORS AND THEIR FLOWERS

	Moth	Flower or Flowers
1.		
2.		
3.		
4.		
5.		
6.		
7.		

Insects and Flowers. Moths are only one kind of insect that visits flowers after the sun goes down. Spend some time watching night-blooming flowers and find out what other insects come to the flowers. A chart similar to the one below will help you keep a record of your observations.

Date	Flower	Insect
1.	night-blooming lilies	earwig, katydid
2.		
3.		
4.		
5.		

The Moth and the Evening Primrose. The group of flowers called "evening primrose" has many members, and they do not all bloom in the evening. For example, sundrop flowers open during the day. Evening primrose *(Oenothera biennis),* as its name implies, unfolds its blossoms at twilight. Find a stand of evening primroses at dusk and observe them for some time. At what time do they open? Do they all open at the same time?

You will discover as the blossoms open that hawkmoths gather and flit from flower to flower as quick as a wink. (See Chapter Note 3.)

Moths and Pheromones. Scientists have discovered that the scent of a female moth is very important in the life of a species. You can discover how powerful that scent is by carrying out a simple investigation. Because the distinction between male and female moths is difficult to determine, trap several moths and put each one in its own box and cover it. After a while, remove the moths from the boxes. If there was a female moth in any of the boxes, the pheromones from that moth will diffuse through the night air and many male moths will fly to her empty box.

If you find many moths flying around a single moth it may be a female, so use it for the investigation. See what happens. (See Chapter Note 4.)

CHAPTER NOTES

1. Moisture and Odor. Smelling is better on a damp night than on a dry night because particles of moisture help carry more particles of odor and they can travel farther.

2. Night-blooming Flowers. Honeysuckle (*Lonicera* sp.) opens its flowers in late afternoon.

Evening primrose (*Oenothera biennis*) has a butter yellow interior. You can see the flower buds of the night to come and the faded blossoms of the night before on the same flower stalk. The flower and the moth have an interesting relationship. Although the flower can self-pollinate, the moth cross-pollinates them and the moth larvae feed on the developing seeds.

Dame's-rocket (*Hesperis matronalis*) releases its sweet fragrance at dusk. Look for it at the edge of woodlands.

Meadowsweet (*Filipendula ulmaria*). A hot, sultry evening after a summer storm is a good time to look for this flower. Its heavy, sweet perfume fills the night air over meadows. Although you can smell meadowsweet during the day, its odor becomes most powerful at night.

3. Primrose and People. Native Americans rubbed oils from evening primrose on aching muscles. Recent research into certain metabolic disorders indicates that oil from evening primrose seed may be a helpful treatment.

4. Pheromones. Pheromones are chemicals secreted by animals and insects that are recognized by members of the same species. These chemicals cause behavioral responses that you can see as well as physiological changes that cannot be observed.

Primer pheromones will announce the presence of a foreign ant in a colony and will cause a response over a period of time. Releaser pheromones also help control the animal's external environment by causing an immediate response in another animal of the same species.

Some animals produce smells (allomones) that can be detected by animals of other species. The skunk is the champion in this category.

CHAPTER 3

Sound

THINGS DO GO BUMP IN THE NIGHT

It's a classic sitcom scene. Three youngsters persuade their parents to let them sleep in a tent in the backyard. After the sun sets, the kids begin to hear the spooky sounds of the night. Rustling leaves and snapping twigs conjure up images of big, hungry bears. Hooting owls seem to be circling overhead. Trees groan in the breeze. Frogs boom out the sounds of a water monster. Insects bounce off the tent. What's going on? The night always seems quiet from their bedrooms, yet outdoors sounds are bombarding them from all sides. Finally, they race into the safety of the house, where their parents await them with cookies and milk.

These children have learned some of the important facts about the wild world after sunset. First and perhaps most important, they have discovered that when our eyesight is not very useful, we become acutely aware of the sounds that we have ignored while our eyes filled our minds with information. Second, they have discovered that the animals of the night produce a great variety of sounds. Why and how night creatures make sounds are explained in many of the following chapters.

First let's examine the nature of sound. You have seen the wonderful effects caused by falling dominoes; each one knocks over its neighbor, causing a moving "wave." Individual dominoes do not travel from one place to another, but mechanical energy is passed from one domino to the next along the chain. Sound travels through the air in a similar way. If someone on the other side of the room drops a book onto the floor, the energy caused by this event strikes air molecules, causing them to vibrate and bump their neighbor molecules. The wave of energy passes from one molecule to another until it reaches your ears. The air molecules do not travel to your ears. Only the energy, in the form of sound, reaches you.

Hearing occurs when this mechanical energy is trapped by our ear flaps (pinnae) and transmitted through our middle ear to our inner ear. Through a complex process the mechanical energy is transformed into electrical energy in the inner ear and sent to the brain. In the section of the brain specialized to process this energy, the vibrations are interpreted as specific sounds.

For communication among members of a species to be effective, signals must be both sent and received successfully; then the message results in appropriate behavior. For example, the scream of a frog about to be devoured by a hungry snake is "understood" by other frogs in the pond, who react by diving for cover. The courtship call of the male woodcock piques the interest of female woodcocks in the area, who then "decide" on their next move.

Although many living things communicate by sending and receiving vibrations and transforming them into a "language" they can understand, there are many notable differences in the way this is done. Some animals are equipped with voice boxes similar to ours, whereas others make noises by rubbing various body parts together. Some produce high-pitched squeaks; others buzz or chirp. Some have songs that encourage us to come closer; others have growls that warn us to keep our distance. As assorted as the sound-producing tricks are, the devices used to receive vibrations from the environment are just as varied. In the activities that follow you will have an opportunity to discover some strategies animals use to communicate with each other through sound.

To better understand the sound-gathering mechanisms of other creatures, let's take a look at our own hearing device. Each of our ears is made up of an outer ear, a middle ear, and an inner ear. The most obvious part of our auditory trio is our external ear flaps, or pinnae. Ear flaps are characteristic among mammals, and in most mammals the ear flaps are movable. You only have to observe a cat or a dog to find out how directional the ear flaps can be. Even though you may have a friend who can wiggle his ears, most human beings don't have this ability. For us to make effective use of our sound catchers, we must tilt the head to one side or the other and move it back and forth.

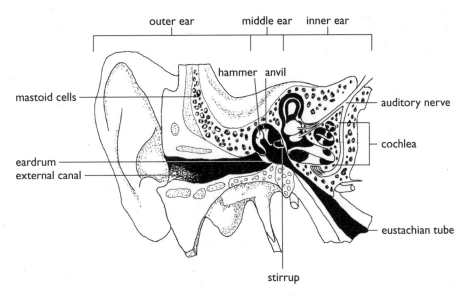

cutaway view of the human ear

The flap, or pinna, picks up sound waves and funnels them into the auditory canal, where they are directed to the tympanic membrane, or eardrum.

The ear canal contains tiny, often prominent, hairs and modified sweat glands that manufacture a waxy secretion. The hairs trap foreign particles from the air much like the hairs in the nose catch dust from the air we breathe. The wax keeps the eardrum soft and pliable, essential to its function. The middle ear contains three little bones (ossicles) called the hammer, anvil, and stirrup because of their resemblance to those objects. One end of the hammer touches the eardrum; the other end connects with the anvil, which connects with the stirrup. The foot plate of the stirrup is attached to the oval window of the inner ear. These little bones make a continuous chain across the air-filled middle ear and are suspended by tiny ligaments that synchronize their movements.

Connecting the middle ear with the nasal cavity is the eustachian tube. Scientists have known about the duct since 1563, when Bartolommeo Eustachio, an Italian who specialized in the study of anatomy, first described the role of this hollow tube in equalizing pressure on either side of the eardrum. When riding in elevators or airplanes, or while driving across mountainous terrain, you probably have felt sudden pressure changes in your eardrums. Chewing gum, yawning, or swallowing helps relieve your discomfort by moving air through the eustachian tube and equalizing pressure on the eardrum.

An intricate system of bony canals and membranous tubes forms the inner ear. It is here that the tiny, delicate organ of hearing is located. The cochlea is a coiled, fluid-filled apparatus about the size of a small fingernail and resembling a snail shell.

Sound vibrations move easily through air, but it is more difficult for them to travel through a dense medium such as water. If sound waves were to travel directly from the outer ear to the fluid-filled inner ear, they would not have enough energy to cause ripples in the fluid. The role of the bones in the middle ear is to amplify the low-energy waves so that they can be transmitted through the fluid of the cochlea.

The inner ear also houses the organs of balance, the semicircular canals. These three interconnected loop-shaped tubes are filled with a thicker-than-water fluid. The job of the semicircular canals is to help us maintain our balance and give us a sense of orientation (where we are in relation to what's around us). They function through the interaction of fluid on hairlike projections that detect changes in body orientation. Each loop has a particular task: one monitors up-and-down motion, another detects forward motion, and the third helps you know if you are moving from side to side. Within the inner ear, the semicircular canals share space with the cochlea and are protected by the hard tissue that makes up the temporal bone of the skull, the bone above your ears.

More primitive animals don't have such complicated hearing systems, but they do have balance organs. You can find these balance mechanisms in the lateral line system of fish, which enables them to detect low-frequency vibrations, turbulence, and pressure changes in the water such as those caused by passing fish. A jellyfish is subject to wave action, but it has an organ of equilibrium called a statocyst that helps the animal maintain its balance. This is especially important for a creature being tossed about in rough seas.

The hearing system of frogs is more developed than that of fish. They have ears that detect airborne sounds, but they lack an external ear. The next

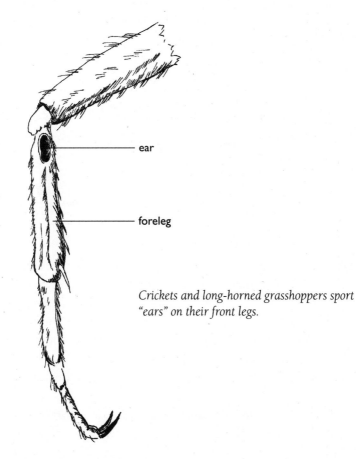

ear

foreleg

Crickets and long-horned grasshoppers sport "ears" on their front legs.

time you examine a frog, look for the disc-shaped "eardrums" just behind the frog's eyes. Scientists have discovered that some frogs communicate by way of sound waves sent through the ground rather than through the air. The disadvantage to these kinds of waves is that they travel only short distances, but there is little danger that frog predators will "hear" them. Snakes, salamanders, cockroaches, and mole rats are also able to communicate in this way.

Crickets and grasshoppers have different, fascinating mechanisms that allow them to communicate with each other. You will have an opportunity to learn a little about their language and the structures they have for "hearing" in chapter 10.

Birds have middle ears complete with cochlea and semicircular canals. The canals are filled with a fluid more dense than water and operate much like the semicircular canals in our inner ears, helping the bird keep its balance and orient itself in space. Interestingly, bird ears are similar to those of crocodiles.

Living things have many effective ways to communicate with others of their own kind. You will begin to explore some of them in the activities that follow. Learning about the diversity of these tricks can be an exciting adventure.

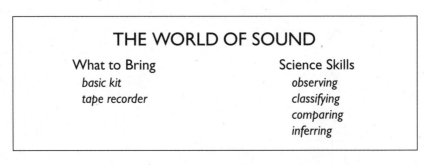

THE WORLD OF SOUND

What to Bring
basic kit
tape recorder

Science Skills
observing
classifying
comparing
inferring

ACTIVITIES

You have heard the varied voices of living things fill the night as they send messages to others of their own kind. You may not have realized that each night their voices begin according to a schedule. Bats, nighthawks, skunks, insects, frogs, and others creatures respond to various cues in the environment such as temperature, humidity, and level of darkness. Some animals become active and vocal early in the evening. Others begin their nightly routine much later. The process is well ordered, not random, and is consistent night after night.

It's important to remember that this is not just a haphazard collection of mammals, birds, amphibians, and insects that we hear; it's a network of life.

As you listen, you will hear a drama of reproduction—of new life—and a drama of survival as predator and prey seek and hide. An owl on the alert listens for mice scuttling through the leaf litter, and a hungry bat follows the sounds reflected from night-flying moths.

Robert Louis Stevenson compared the night sounds to a clock because the hours of the night are "marked by changes in the face of Nature." With the help of some record keeping, you too can discover this audible night clock in your neck of the woods.

As you read other chapters in this book, you will discover more about the vital role of sound in the nighttime world.

A Sound Census. As eye-dependent human beings we forget we can collect information about our world by using our ears. Sit quietly for thirty minutes or so and listen to the night. You will probably be aware of some familiar sounds such as the bark of a dog, the voices of children, or the wail of a cat. Listen for more unfamiliar sounds such as the rustle of a field mouse foraging in the leaf litter, the songs of crickets, or the hoot of an owl.

Keep a record of what you hear and the time you hear it. Repeat this exercise for several nights. (Scientists keep observational records for a long time before they make any general statements about the problem they are studying.) Is there an order to the sounds you hear, or do the noises occur randomly? Did you find a pattern? Is that splash in the pond part of the pattern, or was it simply an anomaly?

Day versus Night. It is said that sounds travel farther at night than during the day. Perhaps this is related to humidity or temperature, or perhaps this is just because we listen more carefully when we cannot see very well. Can you design an investigation that would help you to figure out if sound really travels farther at night?

Wind. Sound is produced by objects vibrating. In the field and forest, grasses, vines, and branches are moved by the breeze, often producing sounds. The pitch and volume of the sounds depend on the size and stiffness of the vegetation, as well as other factors. Listen to the soft whisper of the wind blowing gently through a pine grove. Compare it to the hissing, pulsating winter wind that whips through the woodland. How would you describe the sound of wind blowing through dry leaves? Listen for other voices of the wind and describe them.

Sudden Silence. The night is full of sounds. Some of those sounds are fairly loud like the cricket symphony, but others, like the churring of a foraging skunk, are faint and require us to get close to the source. Some are unexpected, like the snap of a twig or the sudden rustle of leaf litter that can send a wash of adrenaline through us. We screen out much of the noise that bombards us throughout the day. Be alert for new sounds as you listen to the night. Listen for sudden silences. What are their causes? Are these just pockets of silence? Can you make some of the calling stop? How long does it take for the sounds to begin again?

Birds of Dim Light. Listen for the flutelike notes of the wood thrush. You also may hear the ovenbird's flight song, a bubbly jumble of notes that ends in the familiar "teacher, teacher, teacher." Perhaps you will hear the evening song of the eastern wood pewee, which is quite different from its more familiar daytime whistle. Eastern wood pewees are more often heard than seen because they prefer the upper branches of tall shade trees, where their dull colors camouflage them. Bird calls on tape will help you identify these "songs." When did you first hear these calls? Do they occur at about the same time each night?

Battery-powered Bird. The whippoorwill, a bird about the size of a blue jay, is very difficult to spot. It spends the day silently sleeping on the woodland floor among dead leaves, where its mottled brown plumage provides excellent camouflage. At night, a whippoorwill makes itself known through repetitive calling of its name: "Whip-poor-will, whip-poor-will, whip-poor-will." John Burroughs, a famous naturalist, recorded 1,088 continuous calls from one bird. Another recording tallied 1,136 repetitions. Listen for these calls. How many do repetitions do you hear before the bird stops?

When does the bird in your neighborhood begin to call? Is it the same time each night? Does it seem to call from the same location? When does it stop calling?

Bats and Mosquitoes. Many people who feed birds know that cardinals come for the last meal of the day about ten minutes before sunset. As they are retiring at day's end, bats and mosquitoes appear. Do the bats and mosquitoes arrive before or after sunset? Do they come at the same time each night?

Ears and Adaptations. The ears of nocturnal animals show some interesting adaptations. To observe some of these you may have to visit a zoo or wildlife center that keeps live animals. (Museum dioramas could be helpful as well.) Watch the animals as they sit, lie down, or eat. Describe their ear flaps. Are they large or small in relation to the size of the animal's head? Are the ear flaps covered or lined with fur, or are they naked or nearly so? Does the animal move its ear flaps as it rests quietly or as it eats? Do both ear flaps always move in the same direction at the same time? Can the animal direct one of its ear flaps in one direction while the other ear is pointed in another direction? What advantage is this for the animal?

Naked ears are good for picking up sounds. A nocturnal animal with sound-dampening, fur-covered ear flaps would be handicapped as it tried to find prey or avoid a predator.

Dogs and Sounds. Dogs hear very well and can pick up the sound of something approaching long before we do. Spend some time observing a dog. What does it do with its ear flaps as it picks up sounds? Does it move its head or its ear flaps as it tries to figure out where the sound is coming from? Can the dog change the direction of the ear flaps, or must it turn its head?

If you cannot find a dog to watch, observe a cat or a squirrel.

PART 2

THE PLAYERS

CHAPTER 4

Owls

SILENT HUNTERS

Owls have an image problem. For thousands of years people have feared and misunderstood them, associating them with death and misfortune, wars and sad times. Amazingly, similar attitudes, beliefs, and practices surrounding owls have been shared by people of different cultures and separated by vast land masses, expansive oceans, and eons of time.

In 1918 a few adventurous boys in southern France discovered a cave painting depicting a family of snowy owls. Scientists have determined that the mural was painted about 17,000 years ago, the time of the last ice age, and was used in religious or magical ceremonies.

Owls played an important role in ancient Egyptian life, as well. Owl images adorn the tombs of the pharaohs and other sacred places because the ancient Egyptians believed that they protected the dead from the "darkness of the grave." The ancient Greeks were the first to study owls, but their sparse scientific observations were spiced with myth and superstition.

The folklore of Native Americans is also filled with dire references to owls, which were frequently associated with the dead and evildoing. Tribal people believed that owls accompanied dead souls in their journey through the netherworld, but they also believed that owls would protect brave warriors in battle. Hunters often made their arrows with owl feathers in recognition of the birds' predatory skill. In rural Japan and China, images of owls were hung from houses to ward off evil spirits. The voice of an owl in the dark of night was interpreted by tribal people as the voice of a seriously ill person about to die. To understand why owls have evoked such reactions in diverse groups of people, let's look at some of the behaviors and physical characteristics of these feathered beasts.

The owl's habit of working under the black cloak of night and being difficult to find during the day has certainly contributed to its mystique. Of the eighteen species of owls in North America, only four eat insects and hunt by day. Most owls prey on mammals that roam the night—mice, voles, skunks, and even raccoons. Many spend the day sleeping in tree cavities, and those that are active during daylight are difficult to observe because they are well camouflaged—the colors and patterns of owl feathers closely imitate the fissures and plates of tree bark so that when an owl is perched in a tree, it seems to become part of it. The bird's ability to remain absolutely motionless conceals it from even well-trained eyes.

Birds made their debut on the evolutionary stage some 80 million years ago, and the evidence tells scientists that the owl's story began about 60 million years ago. In the process of evolving, owls became nocturnal along with

Almost invisible, this screech owl perches outside its nest.

other bird species, but the first owls separated from the nighttime insect eaters such as the nightjars (whippoorwills) and became predatory.

Another characteristic that has added to the mystery surrounding these birds of prey is their tendency to pierce the night with their strange vocalizations. Unlike songbirds, which sing sweet melodies during mating season, owls hoot, yelp, screech, and mew to define their territories and to attract mates.

Most people describe the voice of the owl as a "whoo-whoo" or "hoot, hoot," or the simple series of "hoo, hoo, hoo" generally associated with that "Halloween" bird, the great horned owl. Such simplification of owl language doesn't accurately describe the variety of cries and calls that are distinct to each owl species. The inquiring "Who cooks for you? Who cooks for you all?" of the barred owl is quite different from the soft, quavering notes of the screech owl (an unfortunate name, indeed). Neither of these calls resembles the sound of hissing snakes made by the barn owl. The tiny saw-whet owl whistles a rapid repetition of "too-too-too," while a dovelike "coo" or catlike "mew" comes from the long-eared owl. If you are unfamiliar with these and other owl voices, hearing them for the first time in the dark of night can be very unsettling. With a single wail an owl can fracture the cold silence of a winter night. What makes owl sounds even more spooky is that you cannot always pinpoint their source; they reverberate through the woodland like formless voices among the naked trees.

Owl noises are not limited to hoots, shrieks, and wails. When frightened, agitated, or protecting their territory, owls rapidly snap their beaks open and shut, producing a loud clacking sound. Beak clacking means, "You have entered my space—get out!" and is a warning worth heeding. These are birds of prey, and they are well designed for attack.

A saw-whet owl swoops silently down from a pine tree.

THE PLAYERS

fringe ————

Fringes on the edges of an owl's feathers break up the flow of air and silence its flight.

Another unsettling aspect of owls is their tendency to appear out of nowhere. Many hunters, scientists, and nightwalkers have been terrified as a hurtling black form silently swoops down in front of their path and disappears into the nearby woods. Noiseless flight is essential to a night stalker. Wings that whistled or squeaked like those of a swan or dove would frighten off nervous, watchful prey. Owls have two features that make silent flight possible—large wings and specially designed wing feathers. Because owls' wings are large for a bird of their body size and weight, they don't have to flap them as often to stay airborne and can maneuver more slowly among the trees and shrubs of forest and field.

The owl's wing feathers have soft, furry fringed edges; the feathers of most other birds are stiff-edged. As the owl flaps its wings, air is trapped between the fine fringes, dampening the noise of the air rushing through the feathers. Feathers on other parts of the owl's body, such as its legs and feet, are similarly

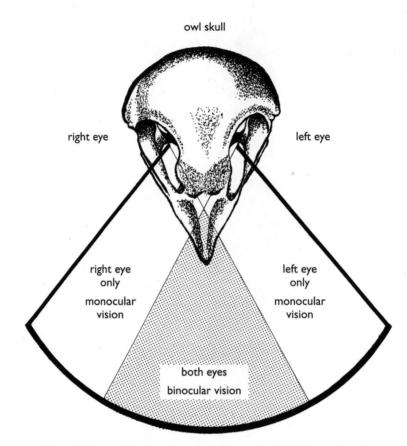

Owls' eyes look straight ahead, giving them a wide field of binocular vision.

soft and contribute to the bird's silent passage through the air. Insect-eating owls such as the burrowing owl and the elf owl don't need this adaptation and consequently have bare legs and feet.

The owl's enormous, blinking eyes are very effective for hunting in the dark, but since they make the owl look almost human, they have contributed to its menacing image. The eyes are so large that they weigh more than the owl's brain—and they are very efficient at gathering light. Owls also have binocular vision, possible because their eyes, like ours but unlike those of most other birds, face forward. When an owl blinks, it moves its feathered upper eyelids rather than the lower lids as other birds do. To see an owl blink at you from a branch in an oak tree can be very unnerving because the placement of the eyes and the unexpected movement of the eyelids is so human.

If you are lucky enough to see an owl in daylight or in the beam of a flashlight, you will discover another unsettling aspect of its eyes—it can stare at you with mesmerizing intensity, never moving its eyes. This is not sinister behavior. Owls simply can't move their eyes within the sockets. To compensate for this potential liability, adaptations in their neck bones (vertebrae) permit owls to swivel their heads about 270 degrees. This means that not only can they look over one shoulder and behind themselves but they can continue to turn their heads and look over the other shoulder as well. This is a survival strategy that protects the owl from attack by its predators.

The eyes are not the only facial feature of the owl that contributed to its ancient reputation—its round, flat face with radiating feathers and sharp, protruding beak resembles a mask, and its head is sometimes topped by a pair of feathery "horns." The "horns," or "ear tufts," are only decorative. The actual ears are oblong slits on the sides of the owl's head, hidden by the feathers of the so-called facial disc. Scientists think that this arrangement of feathers acts as a sound lens, capturing and focusing sound on the ear slits. In an investigation in which the feathers of the facial discs of barn owls were removed, the owls were unable to capture any prey.

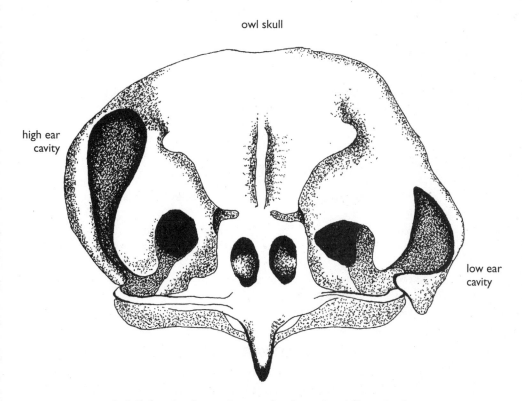

owl skull

high ear cavity

low ear cavity

Owls' left and right ear slits are often located at different levels.

An owl's sound-detection system works much like the giant discs used before the invention of radar to detect enemy aircraft. The discs intercepted the sounds and focused them on a microphone. Stiff facial feathers do this for the owl, which can use this sound mirror to detect the faint footsteps of a mouse in the leaves on the woodland floor. Owls have been observed grabbing their small prey right through a thick cover of snow.

The problem for the owl is not over when it has detected faint sounds—it must also identify the sound's exact location. The owl can do this because its ear slits are asymmetrical. This means that, unlike our ears, the slits are not on the same level on both sides of the bird's head; the ear slit on one side of the head is higher than that on the other side. Because owls have a relatively wide skull, these two slits are widely separated, allowing a lag in the time between when a sound arrives at one side of the head and then at the other side. This enables the owl to determine whether the sound is coming from the right or from the left or from higher or lower than its current location. This system works so well that the barn owl, which has a huge facial disc, can swoop down on mice in absolute darkness using only sound clues.

These behaviors and physical equipment make the owl a magnificent nocturnal hunter. They also set the owl apart from other birds and strike some uncomfortable emotional chords in us. If you have the opportunity, go on an "owl prowl" with your local bird club. You will be guided into the dark woods to hear these masters of the night, and if you are lucky, you will meet an owl eye to eye.

THE WORLD OF OWLS

What to Bring	Science Skills
basic kit	observing
binoculars	recording
glue	inferring
scissors	
a needlelike probe	
a few sheets of white paper	
daring	

OBSERVATIONS

Where to Find Owls. Finding owl roosts can be a challenge for even the most persistent, but knowing where to search and what to look for will increase your chances of a successful hunt. After a night of foraging, owls return to their roosts to sleep. Because owls generally roost in the same trees each night, the trunks are often streaked white with bird lime. Search the bare branches of these marked trees and you may find a sleeping owl or a hollow that the owl calls home.

Other evidence of a roosting owl is a collection of gray, furry two-inch-long bundles at the base of a tree. Called owl pellets, these contain the undigested material from an owl meal and tell you that an owl has been there. If you search dilapidated buildings such as old barns, you will probably find some pellets scattered over the ground or piled beneath beams the owls use to roost. Owls found in these places are generally barn owls.

Your neighbors are another source of information. Let them know you are interested in finding owls, and they may tell you about some roosts they have seen.

Habitats and Owls. Owls are not exclusively woodland birds. Some species prefer open woods with young second-story growth; others prefer open fields, prairies, or marshlands. There are even owls that build their homes in burrows beneath the ground. Knowing these preferences will help you decide which owls to look for in your area. The accompanying chart and range maps might help you.

Owl	Habitat
Screech owl (*Otus asio*)	Small wooded areas, suburbs, orchards
Great horned owl (*Bubo virginianus*)	Almost anywhere except cities
Barn owl (*Tyto alba*)	Abandoned buildings and barns; fields and marshes
Barred owl (*Strix varia*)	Dense woodlands
Great gray owl (*Strix nebulosa*)	Coniferous forests
Saw-whet owl (*Aegolius acadica*)	Dense thickets, likes to roost in evergreens
Long-eared owl (*Asio otus*)	Woodlands close to open fields
Short-eared owl (*Asio flammeus*)	Open fields, meadows, prairies, and marshes
Pygmy owl (*Glausidium gnoma*)	Deciduous and coniferous woodlands
Burrowing owl (*Speotyto cunicularia*)	Prairies and plains

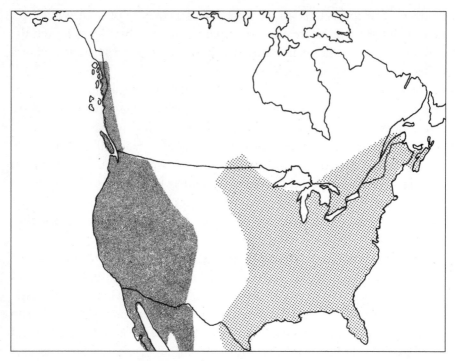

The eastern screech owl (Otus asio) *and the western screech owl* (Otus kennicottii) *were formerly classified as a single species. The range separation is not yet fully known.*

When to Look for Owls. Most owls hunt for food in the dark, but there are a few species that forage during the day and a few others that you can expect to see both by day and by night. The table lists only those owls that cover a wide geographic range and that you are most likely to find.

WHEN THE OWLS PROWL

Day or Night	Day	Night
Short-eared owl	Pygmy owl	Barn owl
Burrowing owl		Long-eared owl
		Great horned owl
		Barred owl
		Short-eared owl
		Burrowing owl
		Screech owl

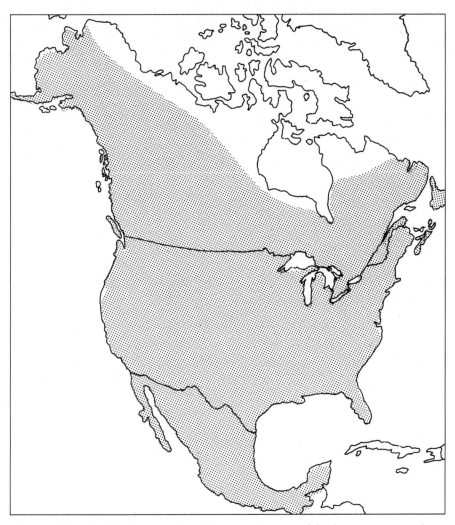

The great horned owl (Bubo virginianus) *ranges over most of the continent, even to the edge of the tundra in central Canada.*

Sounds Made by Owls. One of the best ways to begin to learn about the variety of sounds that owls can make is to listen to tapes of bird sounds. You can find these tapes at nature centers, bookstores, and nature stores.

Owls by Night, Hawks by Day. Owls and hawks are predators that have an ecological relationship with each other. This means that whereas owls hunt predominantly at night, hawks fill their niche during the day. Both birds hunt similar prey species.

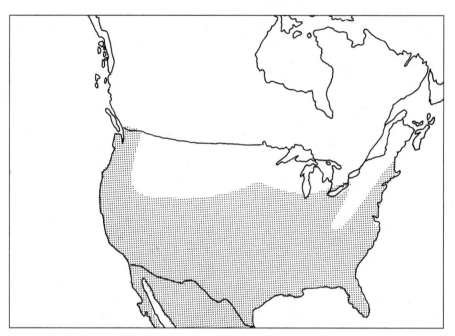

The barn owl (Tyto alba) *can be found nearly worldwide in tropical and temperate regions alike.*

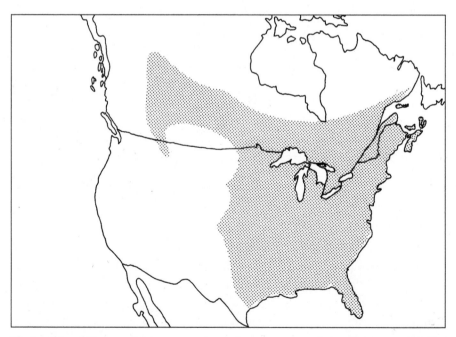

The barred owl (Strix varia) *is common in southern swamps and river bottoms and is also widespread in northern woods.*

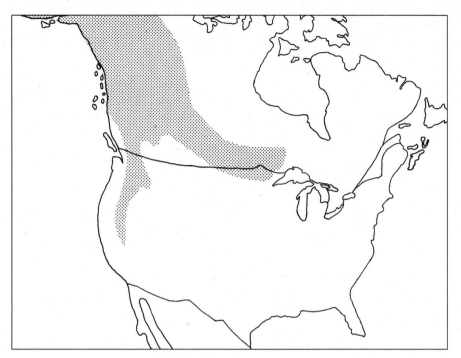

The great gray owl (Strix nebulosa) is found at high elevations in the north and central Sierra Nevada and Rocky Mountains.

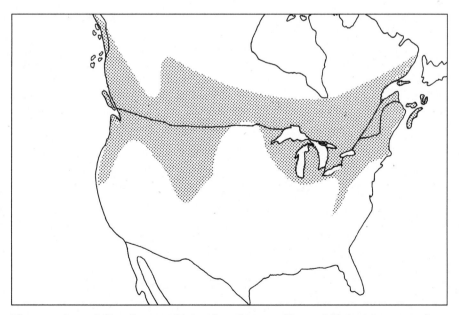

The saw-whet owl (Aegolius acadica) is the only tiny tuftless owl likely to be seen in the central and eastern United States.

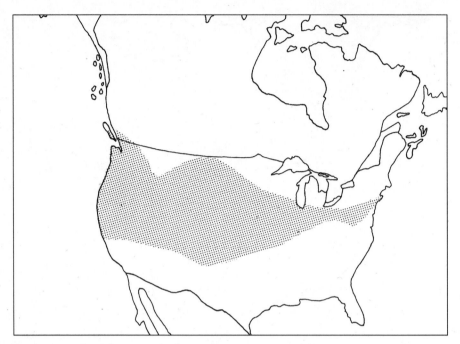

The long-eared owl (Asio otus) *often roosts in groups in woods near open country.*

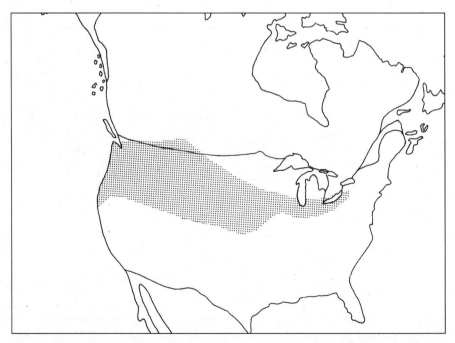

The short-eared owl (Asio flammeus) *may be seen in open country, often before dark.*

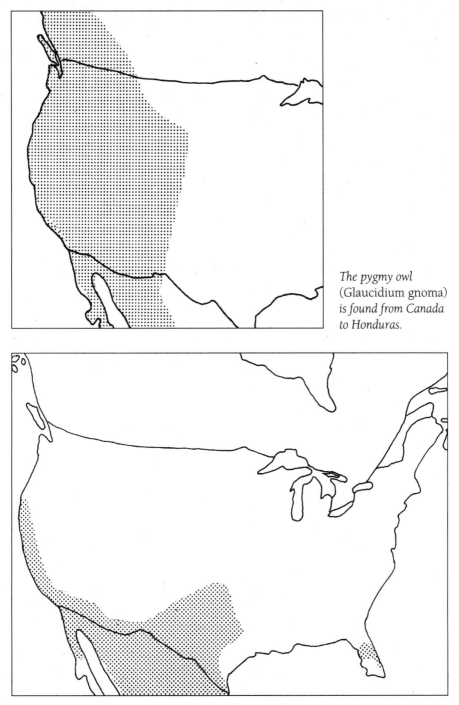

The pygmy owl (Glaucidium gnoma) is found from Canada to Honduras.

The burrowing owl (Speotyto cunicularia) *can be found in the open grasslands and prairies of the western United States, Florida, and south to Argentina.*

The following chart displays some of these relationships. What do you think some of the prey animals are?

Habitat	Owl (by night)	Hawk (by day)	Prey
Open areas, marshlands, grasslands, prairies	Short-eared owl	Northern harrier (marsh hawk)	
Mixed deciduous forests, open woodlands, plains	Great horned owl	Cooper's hawk Red-tailed hawk	
Mature forests, wooded swamps	Barred owl	Red-shouldered hawk	
Prairie, marshland, farmland	Barn owl	Rough-legged hawk	
Woodlands, deciduous forests, farmlands	Screech owl	Sparrow hawk	

Where Is That Owl, Anyway? The call of an owl generally echoes through the woodland. Trying to locate the source of the call can be a frustrating experience, but a method called triangulation can help. You and a friend should stand about fifty feet apart. When you hear an owl call, each of you should shine the beam of a flashlight at the sound. Where the beams of light meet, you will probably find your owl.

Listen to the owls as they speak to each other. How many owls are there?

What Other Creatures Share the Night? Go for a night walk in the woods with a friend and find a quiet spot where you can sit and be comfortable. As you listen to the darkness, you will discover that you are not alone but share the night with a variety of living things. These creatures can be big animals such as deer and foxes; medium-sized critters like skunks,

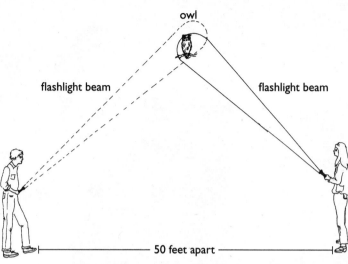

owl

flashlight beam

flashlight beam

├──────────── 50 feet apart ────────────┤

Triangulation can be used to locate an owl.

rabbits, or raccoons; or little animals like mice and voles. Describe the sounds you hear. Does the animal have a lumbering gait, or does it flit from place to place? How fast is the animal moving? How big is it? What clues could you use to determine the animal's size? When you think the animal might be close to you, use a flashlight. You might get a glimpse of some of these nocturnal creatures.

Mobbing. The presence of an owl in the vicinity of songbirds frightens these little birds because they and their young are often preyed on by owls. One of the responses to this fear is to attack the owl. When a squadron of attackers is made up of birds from one or several different species the process is called "mobbing" and usually occurs during the mating season.

Listen for the sound of screeching and scolding birds. Quickly follow the sound and you are likely to come upon a songbird attack against a local owl or hawk.

What species of songbirds are involved in the attack? Can you find chickadees, titmice, warblers, sparrows, hummingbirds, or blackbirds? Are there any crows or jays in the mob? Do other bird species join in the attack once it has begun? Do different species of mobbing birds behave the same way? Do the birds launch a direct attack? Is the attack always accompanied by noise? How close do the attackers get to the owl? Do some types of birds get closer to the owl than other birds during the attack? How do hummingbirds behave?

What is the owl's response to the attack? (See Chapter Note 1.)

Map the Path of a Barn Owl. Barn owls generally begin to hunt just

Small birds often mob a predator in an effort to chase it away.

Barn owls usually use the same path each night for foraging.

before darkness completely enfolds the land. They usually work in pairs unless the female is incubating eggs. Once you have found their nesting place, all you have to do is wait for them to appear. If you can visit this place just before the light of early dawn, you may see them return home.

The path used by the foraging owls is predictable because they use the same route each night. If you have the time and the patience, you can make a map of their nightly path. The map will tell you something about how the prey species of these owls are distributed in an area. (See Chapter Note 2.)

Hunt for Owl Nests. Owls are not tidy housekeepers, and they almost always take over abandoned nests of suitable size made from sticks and dry grasses by hawks, crows, flickers, or small woodpeckers.

Owl	Favorite Nesting Places
Screech owl	Natural tree cavities, especially in apple, oak, or sycamore trees
Long-eared owl	Old tree stumps, deserted crow and hawk nests, rarely on the ground, same nest occupied for successive years
Great horned owl	Deserted nests of large hawks; cliff ledges; deserted tree cavities (in the eastern part of its range)
Barn owl	Not fussy about their home sites; deserted buildings such as churches, granaries, or barns will do nicely in the absence of tree hollows
Pygmy owl	Abandoned woodpecker holes in tree cavities
Burrowing owl	Underground holes they have excavated; even in storm drain pipes
Short-eared owl	On the ground in dugout depressions lined with dry grasses, reeds, and feathers making a platform about two inches off the ground
Saw-whet owl	Abandoned flicker holes found in moist, semidark forests with access to running water
Barred owl	In the northern part of their range they prefer abandoned large tree cavities such as old hawks' nests in pine or hemlock forests; to the south you can find them in similar cavities in mixed hardwood forests and in pure stands of sycamore, sweet gum, willow, or poplar trees

When an owl attacks, its widely spread talons are powerful weapons for hitting and gripping prey.

Owl Talons. If you are fortunate, you may see an owl swoop from the sky and capture its prey. Write a description of the hunt from the time the owl has spotted the prey until it flies away with it. You will have to watch very closely. How does the owl use its wings to stop its forward motion? Its tail? What does it do with its head? How do you think this action affects the owl's vision? How does the angle of its feet change in relation to its body? (See Chapter Note 3.)

The owl's four toes end in razor-sharp talons curved like a cutlass or scythe. When the bird perches on a branch, three of the toes grab from the front while the fourth grasps the branch from behind. When grasping the nape of a prey, the outside toes on the owl's feet swivel toward the back—these two sets of toes oppose one another and are great for grabbing.

EXPLORATIONS

Owl Pellets—Introduction. Owls do not chew their food. If the prey are small, owls will swallow them whole, but if the animals are large (like rabbits), owls will tear them with their sharp beaks into pieces that can be swallowed more easily. Owls can digest the soft body parts of their prey, but their digestive enzymes cannot break down other materials such as fur, feathers, bones, and the chitinous material of insect exoskeletons. These waste materials are pressed into neat bundles by the bird's strong stomach muscles. The bird regurgitates the packages and drops them onto the woodland floor. These pellets, which come in various shades of gray and brown, are two to three and one-half inches long and one inch in diameter. Subtle differences in size, shape, and hue tell the expert which species of owl produced the pellet. Grouse, gulls, swifts, and kestrels also produce pellets, but they are generally more difficult to find and contain only fragments of the birds' meals.

Owl pellets are valuable to ecologists and biologists interested in natural systems because they provide information about which animals various owls are eating, the distribution of owl prey in an area, the number of litters born to the prey each year, the habitat preference of hunting owls, and the sea-

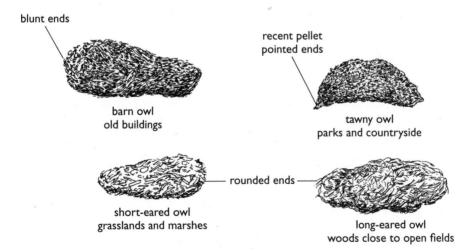

blunt ends

barn owl
old buildings

recent pellet
pointed ends

tawny owl
parks and countryside

short-eared owl
grasslands and marshes

rounded ends

long-eared owl
woods close to open fields

The shape of a pellet and the place where it was found help to identify the species of owl that produced it.

sonal distribution of prey and its effects on owl diets. With this information, scientists can map hunting territories of particular owl species.

Indirect observation is one of the tools scientists use to find out about ecological systems and the organisms that make up those systems. The study of owl pellets is an example of this scientific tool.

Pellet Collecting. This is a great activity to do with a friend. To collect pellets you will have to spend some time hunting in areas where you have heard owls calling. Look for the telltale lime-streaked trees in woodlands and urban parks. You will probably find pellets at the base of some of these trees. Don't forget to look around vacant buildings.

Owl pellets don't smell, and they are not slimy. They are safe to touch. You may find some that are damp, but this is due to mist and rain, not owl secretions. When you find some pellets, put them in a plastic sandwich bag and label it with the location, date, time of day, and weather conditions.

Pellets can collect bacteria and other small organisms, so leave them wrapped in the plastic bag or place them in a sealed container and put them in your freezer for two weeks. When you finish working with the pellets, wash your hands. If you are unable to find any pellets, you can buy them from biological supply houses at a very modest cost.

An Overview of a Pellet. What color is your pellet? What are its length and width? Can you see any objects in the pellet, or is it solid fur? Make a drawing of your pellet.

Inside the Pellet. To discover the secrets held within a pellet, you are going to need a pair of tweezers, a darning needle, and a bowl of water. The pellets are easier to tease apart when wet, and there is less danger of breaking the bones inside. Use a hand lens to find tiny bones you may have overlooked. If you have enough pellets, you might want to try opening a dry pellet. You will be surprised at how tightly packed it is.

With a pair of tweezers, remove the bones from the fur ball and put them on a piece of white paper so that you can keep track of them. Keep the bowl of water on hand to swish the bones clean of debris.

What colors can you detect in the fur? Gray? Black? Brown? White? Other?

Analyze the Pellet Contents. Look for similarities and differences among the bones you find in owl pellets. With the help of the chart below, group bones of the same kind together. How many shoulder blades do you find? How many hip bones? Vertebrae? Hind legs or parts of hind legs? Forelegs or parts of forelegs? Ribs? Do you see any similarities between the bones in your pellets and human bones?

BONES IN THE COLLECTION

Example	Bones	Tally
	skull	
	jaw	
	ribs	
	hip	
	shoulder blade	
	hind legs	
	front legs	
	vertebrae	

(Examples not to scale)

You can disinfect the bones by swishing them in a bleach solution. Don't leave them in the bleach too long or you might damage them.

Bone Display. After you have cleaned and disinfected the bones, make a display of them by gluing them onto a piece of oak tag. This makes it easier to compare them. Look for differences in hip skeletons, skulls, jawbones, and so forth.

Skulls and Legs. Can you infer from the number of skulls in a pellet the number of prey the owl ate? Will the number of legs provide you with the same kind of information? Which is the more accurate predictor for the actual

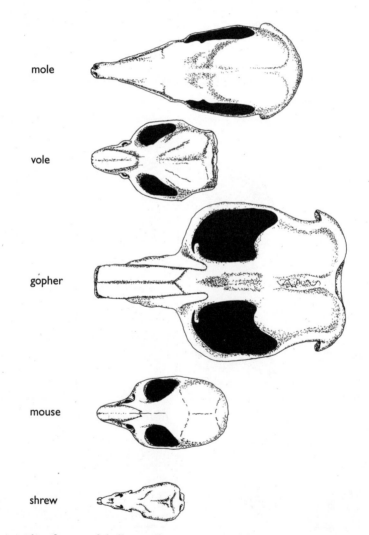

mole

vole

gopher

mouse

shrew

Identification of skulls in pellets is one way of determining an owl's diet.

number of prey eaten by the owl? How many prey do you find in your pellets? In your pellet sample, what is the greatest number of prey in a pellet? The lowest number? The average number of prey?

Make a bar graph to show the relationship between the number of forelegs, hind legs, and skulls. What information does the graph give you about these relationships?

Whose Skull Is That? For the amateur, the key to finding out which animal the owl ate is to examine the skull. With the help of the diagram, determine what mammals are in your pellets. Make a tally of these numbers. Which prey species is present most often? Least often?

If an owl produces one pellet each day, how many of each prey species will the owl eat in a week? A month? A year?

MAMMAL PREY SPECIES

Mammal	Tally
mole	
vole	
gopher	
mouse	
shrew	

EXPLORATIONS FOR THE VERY INQUISITIVE

Does an Owl Diet Change? If you can find a barn owl roost or another steady source of pellets from one owl species, you can find out something about changes in owl diets. To do this you will need to continue collecting owl pellets throughout the year. By identifying the skulls in those pellets, you can find out if prey species change during the year. Is the change seasonal, or are there other reasons for the change in your area, such as habitat loss through the construction of shopping malls, housing developments, and so forth?

Keep a record of rodent species throughout the year. Are different species more active during one part of the year than others?

Owl Boxes. One way to guarantee a supply of pellets is to build an owl box and have owls move in and make it their home. (See Chapter Note 4.)

Food Chains. From your study of owl pellets you can better understand how owls fit into the food web. Draw a food chain for the owl whose pellets

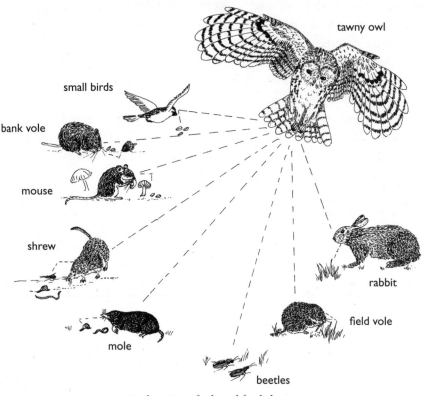

Explanation of selected food chains:
1. *Owl eats rabbit that eats grass.*
2. *Owl eats mole that eats worms and snails.*
3. *Owl eats songbird that eats seeds.*

you have studied. Don't forget that many of the small rodents feed on the seeds from flowering plants (angiosperms). The diagram above illustrates some of these connections.

Injured Owls. As baby owls get ready to leave the nest, they practice jumping from branch to branch. In the process many of them fall out of the tree. While on the ground, they are fed by their parents and are safe from most predators. If you find baby owls in this situation, leave them alone. You don't want to upset the parents.

CHAPTER NOTES

I. Mobbing. Owls will often sit and occasionally blink during the performance and eventually fly into the woods. It's rare that owls retaliate. Pygmy owls are prime targets for mobbing birds. This is no surprise because these daytime hunters prefer a diet of small birds, and downy woodpeckers are a special treat for them. Short-eared owls and screech owls that happen to be around during the day are also prime targets for these attacks. Although the burrowing owl is active during the day, it is not a target for mobbing birds because it does not prey on them.

2. Barn Owl Paths. Barn owls prefer to hunt over open country. They shun forested land, probably because great horned owls find barn owls quite tasty. Great horned owls are strictly nocturnal.

3. An Owl Captures Its Prey. Just before striking the fatal blow, the owl in flight snaps its head back and simultaneously lowers its tail, which functions like the "brakes" (spoilers) on airplane wings to increase drag. The bird's feet stretch forward and its talons grab the prey's neck. This action severs the spinal cord and death quickly follows.

4. Plans for Owl Boxes.

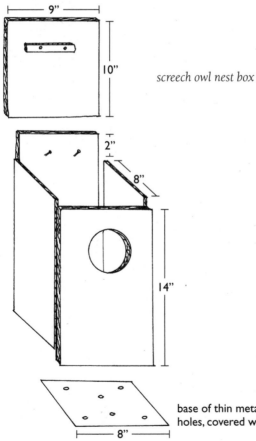

screech owl nest box

base of thin metal with 6 drainage holes, covered with sawdust

CHAPTER 5

Frogs

NIGHT VOICES THAT PROCLAIM SPRING

If you were to ask some friends how they knew that spring had finally arrived, they would probably list melting snow, greening grass, budding trees, and calling birds. Some might also note such nocturnal signs as the nasal "peent" of the woodcock or the song of the cricket. Others would insist that the true herald of spring is the bell-like sound of spring peepers (*Hyla crucifer* or *Pseudacris crucifer*) rising out of the wetlands. As they have done for millions of years, spring peepers and other frogs raise their voices to proclaim the start of breeding season—spring.

Frogs were among the first vertebrates (animals with backbones) capable of spending their adult lives on land. Although their lineage in not clear, it can be traced back to a primitive fish called ichthyostegalia. Somewhere along the evolutionary path, descendants of this fish surrendered many of the characteristics that tied them to the sea. The fossil record does not give the exact time and nature of that transformation; however, the fossils do show that those early frogs shared the world of the steamy early Jurassic forests with plants, dinosaurs, and invertebrates such as scorpions, spiders, and various flying insects.

Today, there are 3,800 known species of frogs worldwide, 82 of which live in North America. Frogs are amphibians, which means that in the course of their lifespan they lead a "double life," first in water and then on land. As eggs and larvae they are bound to a watery existence in freshwater ponds, streams, lakes, or even puddles, but then as adults they adapt to life on land. Scientists place frogs in a special group of amphibians called *anurans*. The word means "without tail" and distinguishes frogs from salamanders and caecilians.

There is nothing like a warm, rainy April night to start frogs calling in their many voices. In early spring we hear males making "advertisement calls" as they define territorial boundaries and alert females to their presence. "Aggressive calls" are made when a male frog spies another male trespassing in his territory. Such intrusions are generally settled peacefully, with the intruder hopping off unharmed. Once territories have been established and females have arrived, the males sing their "courtship calls." If you live close to some pristine wetlands, listen for these three types of calls, as well as the calls of various frog species. Individual frogs can be identified by slight differences in their voices, but this requires very careful listening over a period of time.

Once a female frog has selected her mate from a chorus of competing males, the two join in an embrace called *amplexus,* in which the male grabs

Having found a mate, the male frog grasps her behind her forelimbs, enabling him to fertilize the eggs as they are laid. This embrace is called amplexus.

the female with his forelegs and hooks his thumbs under her front legs. While in this position the female lays her eggs, and the male releases huge quantities of sperm into the water. This process, called external fertilization, may seem rather haphazard, but it has been extremely successful in producing continuous generations of frogs.

You are likely to hear a breeding pond before you see it; it will resound with splashing water and grunting, squawking, hiccupping, yelping, kicking, and squirming frogs. In the confusion, a male frog sometimes embraces something other than a willing female and one of the frogs will sound the alarm in the form of a "release call." There is so much bedlam in a breeding pond that male frogs have been known to hug almost anything that moves, even a human hand.

Once successful breeding has occurred, fertilized eggs are deposited in safe places, which vary according to the species of frog. For example, the eastern spadefoot toad prefers to deposit its eggs in small ponds created by torrential rains. It doesn't matter that these ponds evaporate quickly because it takes only two weeks for the eggs to develop into toads. Bullfrogs (*Rana catesbeiana*) choose more permanent bodies of water, and green frogs (*Rana clamitans*) live in bogs, swamps, and marshes. Frogs usually deposit their eggs in clusters, and toads lay single or double strands of eggs. Look for these long strands in the vegetation along the shallows of permanent ponds or lakes.

A single frog can produce huge quantities of eggs. Gray tree frogs (*Hyla*

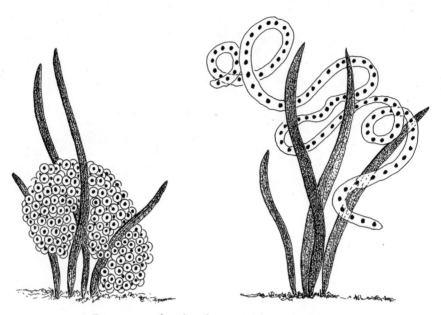

Frog eggs are found in clumps; toad eggs, in strands.

versicolor) lay about 2,000 eggs in small, mucus-coated packets, with 6 to 45 eggs in each packet. The American toad (*Bufo americanus*) deposits between 2,000 and 9,000 eggs in double strands a few feet long. Another variation in egg laying is illustrated by the bullfrog, which lays between 10,000 and 20,000 eggs in a gigantic gelatinous envelope that can spread two to four feet across the water's surface. Mucous covers the two envelopes that protect each of the 1,000 to 3,000 eggs laid by the green frog. Because frog eggs are so vulnerable, most of the eggs and larvae are devoured by predators such as fish, other tadpoles, small mammals, snakes, wading birds, and insects.

Young frogs hatch from their eggs as tadpoles. Generally speaking, neither eggs nor tadpoles are dependent on parental care, so adult frogs are free from the tasks of brooding eggs and feeding the young. Tadpoles survive by exploiting the energy-rich environment of the pond, puddle, or roadside ditch where they live. As they swim, their movement stirs up decaying plant material from the bottom of the pond, nutritious food for hungry tadpoles. The tadpoles' diet helps to extend the life of the pond by cleaning it: without the tadpoles to eat this plant matter, the bacteria of decay would deplete the pond water of oxygen. A pond without oxygen cannot support life-forms; it is dead.

Tadpoles have very large heads, necessary to house the complex filtering system used to strain food from the water. This system acts as a pump, regulating the amount of water that enters the tadpole's mouth. If the pond water is dense with food, a smaller amount of water is admitted, much like a person will take in a larger mouthful of broth than of thick stew. The filtering mechanism enables tadpoles to live in water so turbid that you cannot see them or in a pond so clear that the water looks empty of food.

The length of the tadpole phase varies with frog species and environmental factors. Within a species, the time spent as a tadpole also can vary with geographic location and water temperature. For example, spring peeper tadpoles take as long as 90 to 100 days to develop in the northern part of their range, but tadpoles of the same species living in Florida will become frogs in as little as 45 days. Scientists studying the larvae of green frogs developing in the ponds of Michigan discovered that these tadpoles show a similar response to environmental temperature. The tadpoles that hatched from eggs deposited early in the season became frogs in about 80 days, but those developing from eggs laid later in the summer generally stopped growing when the cold weather arrived and sought the warmth of the pond mud, where they spent the winter. The tadpole stage for this group could last as long as 360 days. A tailed frog (Ascaphus truei) living in the northwestern United States holds the record at 1,080 days in tadpole stage.

Some frogs live for as long as nine years, but most live about four. Therefore, frogs living in cold climates need some strategies for surviving the winter. American and spadefoot toads sleep in burrows beneath the earth; wood frogs and gray tree frogs (Hyla versicolor) prefer to overwinter on the forest

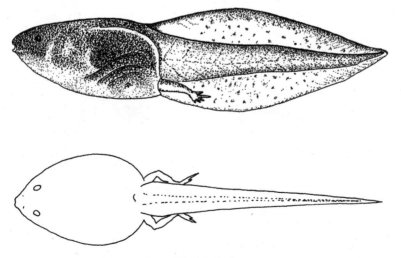

wood frog tadpole
(Rana sylvatica)

life cycle of a frog

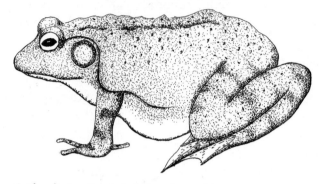

6. The plant-eating tadpole has changed into an insect-eating frog—an adult capable of reproducing.

1. The female lays soft, jelly-covered eggs in the water of a pond, and they are fertilized by the male.

5. Gills are replaced with lungs; the mouth and eyes change and the tail is absorbed.

2. A tiny, fishlike tadpole hatches from an egg.

3. The tadpole breathes through feathery gills that grow on each side of the head. These quickly disappear, to be replaced by internal gills.

4. The hind legs grow first. The front legs grow under the skin and then break through.

floor or in rock crevices covered by leaf litter. Green frogs find shelter on the bottoms of ponds, lakes, or streams, whereas northern leopard frogs snuggle into the soft ooze of streambeds, lakes, and ponds. Scientists know a great deal about the breeding life of many frog species but little about the way they spend the rest of their year.

The life cycle of frogs is called *complete metamorphosis,* which means they pass through egg, larva (tadpole), and adult phases. During the egg and larva stages, they are dependent on water. Some frog species, however, lay their eggs on the ground and do not pass through a water-dependent tadpole stage. Some scientists believe that these species illustrate stages in evolutionary development from water-dependent creatures to those that are completely land dwellers. They estimate that every major frog family has some of these rebellious members that no longer deposit their eggs in the water or produce tadpoles. Instead, small frogs of the species hatch directly from the eggs. The life cycle of these frogs more closely resembles the incomplete metamorphoses of crickets and grasshoppers than that of their anuran cousins. Don't expect to find these rebels in your local pond, though—they live in the tropics where they are not subject to the stresses associated with seasonal change.

Adult frogs must live near water to reproduce, thus water remains essential to the success of the species. During the breeding season they need to mate and deposit their eggs in water because frog eggs are wrapped in a gelatinelike material that easily dries out, rather than a calcium case or leathery shell like bird or turtle eggs.

Although most adult frogs do not drink, all frogs absorb water through their permeable skins, especially the abdominal skin. Some frogs sit for some time during the day in small puddles to replace the water lost through their skin or used in metabolism. Frogs of one species counter water loss by secreting a waxy substance and rubbing it on themselves. Tree frogs have evolved another strategy: they spend the hottest part of the day with their abdomens pressed against the bark of a tree, which minimizes water loss through their permeable abdominal skin. It could be that the problem of water loss is a factor in making frogs creatures of the night, because the night is cooler and more moist. The daytime sun can make it dangerous for frogs to be out.

Herpetologists—those who study the life and times of frogs—are becoming more and more concerned about the amphibians' future. The reports from 1989 and 1990 conferences held by the World Congress of Herpetology and by the Biology Board of the National Research Council cite an alarming worldwide decline in some frog species. Though scientists agree that frogs have had to cope with predators and variations in rainfall, they point out that

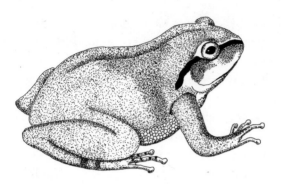

Pacific tree frog
(Hyla regilla)

because frogs absorb moisture through their skin, they are susceptible to pollutants dissolved in the water such as insecticides and pesticides. These chemicals are leached from the land as rain and melting snow drains into frog breeding ponds. Frogs are also gravely affected by acid rain. Habitat destruction through the draining of wetlands for homes and agriculture by humans is another cause of their decreasing numbers, and frogs are killed by cars, generally on roads that separate breeding pools from winter resting places.

Frog voices calling from bogs and swamps as soft rains fall on the still-cold earth stir a sense of hope and of regeneration every spring, but there may come a time when we won't hear those magical sounds. Frogs, like the birds, are warning us that there is a problem with the environment; these beautiful creatures are telling us that something is very wrong in the frog pond.

THE WORLD OF FROGS

What to Bring	**Science Skills**
basic kit	*observing*
dip net	*recording*
large Ziploc bag	*measuring*
gallon jar	
tape recorder	
dedication	

OBSERVATIONS

Putting Anurans in Order. People tend to lump all frogs into a few simple categories—pond frogs versus toads, big frogs versus little frogs—but the world of nature is much more complicated than that. Even in the world of the frogs it is beautifully diverse. Scientists have organized frogs into several groups: tailed frogs, narrow-mouthed toads, spadefoot toads, true toads, cricket frogs, chorus frogs, tree frogs, and true frogs. The activities in this chapter focus on a few of the most available frogs in each major group, as follows:

- Spadefoot toads—eastern spadefoot toad (Scaphiopus holbrooki)
- True toads—American toad (Bufo americanus)
- Tree frogs—spring peeper (Pseudacris crucifer), gray tree frog (Hyla versicolor)
- True frogs—eastern wood frog (Rana sylvatica), northern leopard frog (Rana pipiens), green frog (Rana clamitans), bullfrog (Rana catesbeiana)

These representative frogs have a wide range east of the Rocky Mountains. You can find other species in your locality by consulting a field guide to amphibians. The specific habitats preferred by these frogs are outlined in the chart that follows.

Frog	Habitat
Eastern spadefoot toad (Scaphiopus holbrooki)	Gravelly, sandy, or loamy soils of dunes, farmlands, forests, and meadows
American toad (Bufo americanus)	Diverse, dry habitats including meadows, suburban backyards, mountain forests
Spring peeper (Pseudacris crucifer)	Low-growing shrubs near temporary pools and inland wetlands, floodplains
Gray tree frog (Hyla versicolor)	Trees and shrubs near temporary woodland wetlands
Eastern wood frog (Rana sylvatica)	Damp woodlands, shaded wooded hillsides, meadows
Northern leopard frog (Rana pipiens)	Damp meadows, fields, orchards, brackish marshes
Green frog (Rana clamitans)	Wetlands, along the edges of streams and ponds
Bullfrog (Rana catesbeiana)	Permanent bodies of water, ponds, lakes

When Some Frogs Call. The chart below identifies the months when you can expect to hear the breeding calls of some frogs and toads. Listen for the calls of the frogs in your area and make a similar chart for them. If you do this for several seasons you will notice patterns that will help you predict when they will arrive each year. When there are departures from the pattern, you can explore possible explanations such as an extremely cold winter or habitat destruction. Scientists look for patterns in animal behavior and investigate changes. Frequently, records kept by nonprofessionals are helpful in finding trends and causes.

BREEDING CALLS

Southern range is indicated by ⊢—S—⊣; *northern, by* ⊢···N···⊣.

Frog	Breeding Season
American toad (*Bufo americanus*)	Southern: March–June; Northern: April–June
Spring peeper (*Pseudacris crucifer*)	Southern: February–May; Northern: May–August
Gray tree frog (*Hyla versicolor*)	Southern: April–September; Northern: April–June
Eastern wood frog (*Rana sylvatica*)	Southern: February–March; Northern: February
Northern leopard frog (*Rana pipiens*)	Southern: April–June; Northern: June–October
Green frog (*Rana clamitans*)	Southern: April–September; Northern: June–August
Bullfrog (*Rana catesbeiana*)	Southern: April–September
Spadefoot toad (*Scaphiopus holbrooki*)	Southern: March–July

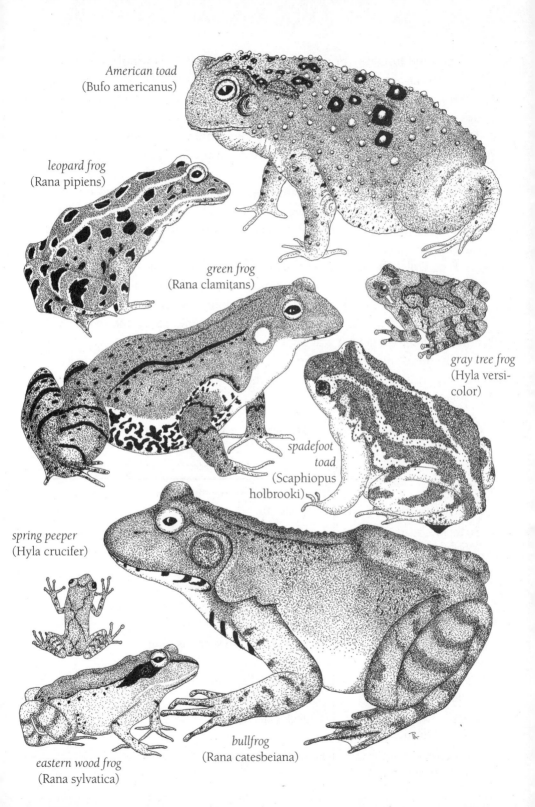

American toad
(Bufo americanus)

leopard frog
(Rana pipiens)

green frog
(Rana clamitans)

gray tree frog
(Hyla versi-
color)

spadefoot
toad
(Scaphiopus
holbrooki)

spring peeper
(Hyla crucifer)

eastern wood frog
(Rana sylvatica)

bullfrog
(Rana catesbeiana)

Rain and humidity bring out the frogs. If the night is windless, so much the better. Listen early in the spring for the calling that marks the beginning of the frogs' annual trek from winter hideouts to their breeding places. Once this migration begins, you can expect the calling to continue into summer. Throughout this period you may see hundreds of frogs hopping across country roads because these roadways cut through the bogs, swamps, and other inland wetlands frogs use for breeding.

If you are not able to locate any frog ponds, ask the naturalists at a local nature center or museum or contact a local group such as the Audubon Society. Members of your local or regional herpetological society are also excellent resources.

Frog Calls. The most accurate way to identify a frog call is to see the vocalist in action, but this is not always possible. A good substitute is to listen to recordings. With the help of modern technology, scientists have recorded frog calls in the field and you can use these at home. Sometimes your local library will have a tape or will get it if you request it.

The following table describes frog calls as compiled by field investigators. It is very difficult to put animal sounds into print, but perhaps this listing will help you.

FROG CALLS

Frog	Sounds
Bullfrog (Rana catesbeiana)	Deep hum or drone, "burr woom," "jug-o-rum," "ooohoom"
Spadefoot toad (Scaphiopus holbrooki)	Deep, explosive, nasal "waank" or "waagh"
Green frog (Rana clamitans)	Banjolike, explosive single note or a series of plunks descending in scale
Spring peeper (Pseudacris crucifer)	Whistlelike, high peep, slurred, higher pitch at the end, 1-second intervals.
Gray tree frog (Hyla versicolor)	Brief, hoarse, 2–6 seconds long
American toad (Bufo americanus)	High-pitched and musical, 5–30 seconds, has a distinct flutelike quality
Eastern wood frog (Rana sylvatica)	"Quack," like a duck
Northern leopard frog (Rana pipiens)	Snorelike croaks

There are those who say that frog calls lack melody, but all agree that the calls have character. Make a tape recording of frog calls to help you decide. (See Chapter Note 1.)

Sneak Up on a Frog. Frogs will immediately be quiet if they detect your footsteps as you approach their calling area. How close can you get to them before they stop calling? Do they all stop their calling at once? If you wait quietly at the edge of the pond, they will resume their calls. How long does it take for this to happen? Do they all start up together, or do they seem to have a leader? Can you map out the locations of leaders and followers?

To Catch a Frog. You need very little equipment to capture a frog. Your bare hands are very good tools, but you may prefer to use a scoop net. (See Chapter Note 2.) The best resource person you can possibly find is a twelve-year-old who lives near a pond. If you are collecting at night, a flashlight with a strong beam is important. When you have the frog in hand, put it into a Ziploc bag and seal it without removing the air. Be sure to include a damp paper towel in the bag to provide moisture for the frog until you have a chance to observe it.

You will notice that frogs face the water when they sit by the edge of a pond. If you put your net in front of the frog, it will be startled and leap into your net.

Is It a Frog or a Toad? It's easy to tell frogs and toads from other amphibians such as salamanders and newts. What is not so easy is to separate frogs from their closer relatives, the toads, as the terms *frog* and *toad* often cause some confusion. It is easiest to make the distinction if you remember that *frog* is an umbrella term that includes all hopping or leaping amphibians, including toads. In other words, toads are a type of frog. The following are a few guidelines that will help you to decide which creature you've captured.

Did you find the critter in a moist habitat such as a marsh, pond, or swampy area? Is it slim with smooth skin and long slender legs? Does it move quickly and leap great distances (greater than its body length)? Did you find it near others of its kind? If you have answered yes to these questions, you probably have caught a frog.

If you found the animal by itself in a drier habitat, such as woodland, meadow, or suburban yard, and thick, bumpy skin covers its plump body, it's a safe guess that you have captured a toad. Prominent bony ridges on top of their heads (cranial crests) and conspicuous swelling behind their eyes (parotid glands) are other marks of toads.

Toads also are known for their sluggish movements, and with stubby legs they hop rather than leap as frogs do. Some frog species such as the gray tree frog have rough skin, which may lead you to believe they are toads, and other frog species may even look like toads—but their long legs and moist skin are good clues to their identity.

TOAD IDENTIFICATION

American toad (*Bufo americanus*)	Large, slow moving Reddish brown Large red warts One large wart in each spot on back Underside spotted with black
Common toad (*Bufo woodhousei*)	Smaller, more agile Greenish gray Small dark green warts Several warts in each spot Underside generally creamy white
Spadefoot toad (*Scaphiopus holbrooki*)	No bony crests over eyes Small, round parotids Conspicuous black, bony "spades" on each hind foot Smooth skin

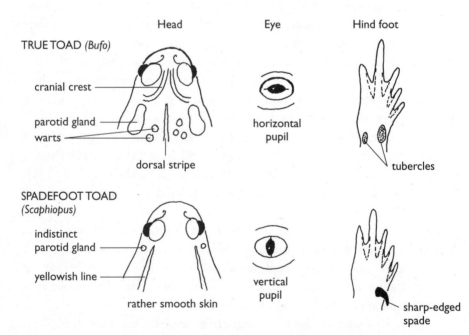

comparison of the true toad and the spadefoot toad

FROG IDENTIFICATION

TREE FROGS (*Hyla* spp.): Swollen discs on tips of toes, toes not webbed

Spring peeper (*H. crucifer*)	Has "x" on its back 1 inch long Light ash gray to light brown
Gray tree frog (*H. versicolor*)	Ash gray Yellow-white spot below eye Rough skin

TRUE FROGS (*Rana* sp.): Seldom found far from water. Many have two ridges (dorsolateral folds) of skin that begin behind the eye and run down on either side of the back. All have webbed toes.

Bullfrog (*R. catesbeiana*)	Largest frog, 6–8 inches long Large mouth Color dusky, mottled Bars of dark color on legs No dorsolateral folds
Green frog (*R. clamitans*)	Small Leaps widely into water when disturbed, often "screaming" Dorsolateral folds Bright green head and shoulders Shades to dusty brown olive on back
Wood frog (*R. sylvatica*)	Small, slender Very long hind legs Pronounced dorsolateral folds Chocolate brown or fawn colored Wears a "face mask" Spends a lot of time away from water
Northern leopard frog (*R. pipiens*)	3–5 inches long Hunts insects in grassy meadows Eardrum (tympanum) almost size of eye Dorsolateral folds Head somewhat pointed Large light-bordered spots on back

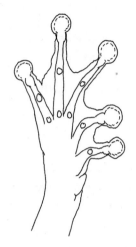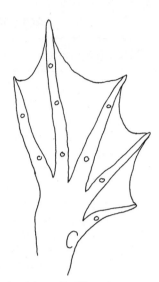

The hind feet of tree frogs have adhesive discs on toes, which help them cling to twigs and bark.

The hind feet of bullfrogs have extensive webs; fourth toe protudes well beyond other toes.

Additional Observations. Almost everyone knows a frog when he sees one, and even small children can tell us that frogs have bulging eyes, wide mouths, and front legs shorter than their hind legs. What may not be so widely known is the way their tongues work. The long, sticky tongue of a frog is attached at the front of its mouth rather than the back, which allows it to do a remarkable thing. Like a fly fisherman casting his line, the frog can flip its tongue into the air and snare a passing insect with amazing speed and efficiency.

Look closely at the frog's eyes. How does it blink its eyes? Does it have eyelids? (See Chapter Note 3.)

Frogs have eardrums, or tympanic membranes, which are round and often a different color than the frog's skin. Look for them behind the eyes. In some frog species you can distinguish the males from the females by the size of the eardrum relative to the eye. If the eardrum is larger than the eye, the frog is a male; if the eardrum is about the same size as the frog's eye, then the frog is a female.

Look at the area behind the frog's eyes. Do you see a conspicuous swelling behind each eye? These are the parotid glands, which toads use to produce toxic chemicals that are distasteful to predators. When threatened, a toad will lower its head to the level of its abdomen, so that when the predator attacks, it will grab the parotids, thus getting a mouthful of foul-tasting, toxic

The frog has a long, sticky tongue attached to the front of the mouth. When an insect flies by, the frog's tongue is propelled out for an instant to grab it.

chemicals. Some frogs, such as the northern leopard frog, similarly secrete acidic fluids that irritate the mucous lining in the predator's mouth.

What color is your frog? Is the color uniform throughout the frog's body? Are there areas that are light in color and others that are dark? Where is the least amount of color? Where is the most color? What advantage do you think this pattern of coloration or shading has for the frog? (See Chapter Note 4.)

The frog you have caught is beautifully designed for living in the water. How do its legs and feet help it to thrive in that environment? Are all feet equally webbed? Can you think of a reason for this? Do the front feet have the same number of toes as the hind feet?

Spadefoot toads are equipped with a special hard, crescent-shaped spade at the heel of each hind foot, an adaptation the toad uses for digging back-

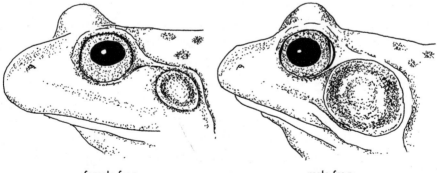

female frog　　　　　　　　　　**male frog**

Frogs do not have exterior ears. The eardrum lies on the surface behind the frog's eyes. Many times eardrums of males are larger than those of females.

wards into its burrow beneath the sandy soil. Young spadefoot toads must make their burrows in very soft, crumbly soil because their spades are soft.

What is its general body shape? How is this an advantage for a creature that spends a great deal of time in the water?

Compare the frog skeleton with a human skeleton. You will notice that frogs don't have ribs. Look for other differences and similarities.

Getting to Know a Frog. One of the most rewarding aspects of frog watching is that you can learn to identify individuals. This kind of identification is important to scientists because it helps them find out such things about a frog as how far it roams, what its territorial boundaries are, and how long it lives. One investigator discovered that an American toad (*Bufo americanus*) lived in his backyard for nine years.

Although frogs and toads of the same species will look similar to each other, you can learn to recognize individual differences in color and pattern design. With practice you will know whether the frog in the garden on one night is the same frog that appears there on other occasions. To do this, you will need to make careful records of each of the frogs you find. Look carefully and record the pattern of color on each frog that you are observing.

Drawings and close-up photographs are additional tools that will help you discriminate among the individuals you find. Add the illustrations to your permanent field collection.

Herpetologists use a method called *toe clipping* to help them identify individual frogs. This procedure does not cause the frog much distress, and the clipped toe will regenerate. For more information on toe clipping, consult *The Amphibians* by Ray and Patricia Ashton.

Photographing Anurans. To add interest to frog watching, you can photograph your subjects in their natural habitat. Because most frogs are quite small and are active at night, you will need some close-up or telephoto lenses and flash equipment. Taking pictures of frogs requires tremendous patience, but the rewards are great. A staged photograph with a captive animal will add interest to your collection, and photos will enrich your field notes.

Observing Food Chains and Webs. Frogs and toads eat invertebrates. Most of these are insects, but spiders, ants, and even earthworms have a place in the anuran diet. Thus, adult frogs and toads are predators. The prey need to be moving in order to activate the feeding response in frogs. You can observe this if you sit quietly beside a frog pond in the twilight. Watch carefully, and you may witness a frog capture a dragonfly or other large insect with its tongue.

Frogs and toads are also delicacies for many other animals. As you spend time around the frog "hot spots," look for the creatures that prey on them. You may be on hand to see some food chains at work. Some frog predators include skunks, turtles, hognosed snakes, garter snakes, wading birds such as green herons, fish, and small mammals such as weasels, raccoons, and muskrats. Even domestic cats and dogs may help themselves to a frog or two.

While you are observing the food chains that involve frogs, look for those in which tadpoles are among the players. Newts, fish, water beetles, and water scorpions are a few tadpole predators.

Flashlight Hunt. The most productive time to hunt for frogs and toads is after a heavy rain. Because many frogs and toads reflect light from their eyes, they will be easier to find if you hold a flashlight at eye level and shine the beam in the direction of the pond or the frog sounds. You may have seen eye shine of dogs or cats reflected in headlight beams. Perhaps you have seen this phenomenon in photos you have taken of your dog while using a flash-bulb—the dog's eyes appear red. Bullfrogs are especially easy to locate by this method, as their eyes shine an opalescent green. (See Chapter Note 5.)

EXPLORATIONS

Observing Life Cycles. Frogs pass through a complete metamorphosis as they develop. This means that as adults they do not resemble the creatures that hatched from the eggs. You can observe the life cycle of a frog from egg to adult by setting up a simple aquarium and putting some frog eggs in it.

Eggs. Frogs lay their jelly-coated eggs in fresh water. Look for them in a pond, puddle, bog, swamp, or any other wet area where frogs breed. You can even find frog spawn (fertilized eggs) in roadside ditches that have been filled by spring rains. Look for the gelatinous masses often tangled in pond vegetation. The water causes the protective jelly to swell, so it's not unusual to see a mass of frog eggs as large as a football. If you have ever tried to pick them out of the water, you know that spawn is very slippery. The advantage for the frogs is that slippery eggs are not easy for predators to grab. The egg masses of some species have such buoyancy that they will float in water. Some tree frogs (*Hyla* sp.) deposit their tiny eggs singly or in small clusters that are difficult to find.

Toad eggs are covered with waterproof material and laid in long strands, sometimes double strands. Look for them along the shallows of ponds or lakes. (See Chapter Note 6.) If you can watch the development of a frog starting at the egg stage, you can observe a tadpole as it becomes an adult.

If you can find some eggs, scoop up a few and put them into a wide-mouthed container. Three or four eggs are enough. When they hatch you can transfer the tadpoles to a larger container (see below). Because tadpoles are sensitive to chlorine and the iron that leaches from water pipes, be sure to use pond water rather than tap water for your aquarium.

Tadpoles (Larvae). Although you have probably seen tadpoles swimming in ponds, you may not have observed them in an orderly way. Systematic observation is a very different way of seeing. A good way to begin systematic observation is to capture one or two tadpoles and observe their structure and their behavior. You can scoop tadpoles out of the pond with a fine mesh net, available in any shop that sells home aquarium supplies. Wear a pair of old sneakers, as you may need to wade into the water.

After capturing the tadpoles, put them into a large container that allows them to swim freely. A wide-mouthed gallon jar is sufficient for two or three tadpoles. Your enthusiasm may push you to take more, but resist the urge to do so unless you plan to use an air pump and a larger container. Add enough water from the pond where you found the tadpoles so that the jar is about three-quarters full. Place the temporary aquarium in a bright area, but avoid direct sunlight. This will give the algae—the tadpoles' food—sufficient light for growth. Don't try to clean the pond water by straining out the tiny particles of dead and decaying plant material, because the tadpoles eat this material as well.

Details of Tadpole Development. A good way to continue your systematic observation of tadpoles is to record daily observations about their structure and behavior in a journal and sketch the tadpoles in different phases of life.

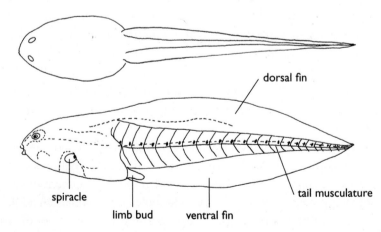

The dotted lines indicate the location of lateral line sense organ on this typical tadpole.

Write a description of a tadpole. What is it doing? With the help of a hand lens, you can discover how a newly hatched tadpole hangs on to plants. What is happening to the tail? Look for the feathery external gills on either side of the tadpole. How do you think it breathes? When do the external gills disappear? When do the hind legs appear? Does the tadpole seem to be gulping air at the water's surface? What is a possible explanation for this behavior? Did your tadpole stop eating? What might be happening?

If you have several tadpoles in a large aquarium, do they stay together (as in a school), or do they swim and eat singly? Do they tend to stay hidden in vegetation? Describe their camouflage. (See Chapter Note 7.)

TADPOLES

Species	Tadpole to Frog	Adult Lifespan
American toad	35–70 days	5–10 years
Common toad	40–60 days	5 years plus
Eastern spadefoot	48–63 days for early broods 16–20 days for late broods	5 years plus
Wood frog	1–70 days	3 years plus
Green frog	1–2 years	5 years plus
Northern leopard frog	63–84 days	3 years plus
Bullfrog	4 months–2 years	6 years plus
Gray tree frog	50–60 days	Unknown
Spring peeper	45–60 days	3 years plus

Frogs in a Terrarium. Frogs can be kept in a terrarium for a short period of time without suffering harm, but because toads are less dependent on water, you may want to use them instead. When you are handling a frog be sure your hands are wet, because hot, dry hands can harm the frog's delicate skin.

You can use a ten-gallon or larger aquarium for adult frogs. Put a rectangular plastic food-storage container into the aquarium and fill it with pond water. A two-cup size will work well. To supply the frog with fresh water, simply remove the container, clean it, and fill it with water.

Into the remaining space put some gravel and cover it with potting soil. Add woodland litter such as a few rocks, some moss, pieces of bark, small branches, and twigs. Finish your temporary frog habitat by placing a piece of screening over the top of the tank to prevent the frog from leaping out.

To feed your frog, you must supply it with live, active insects. A frog will not eat anything that does not move, no matter how hungry it may be. If you give it flying, wiggling insects such as crickets, flies, moths, caterpillars, slugs, snails, and worms, the frog will eat.

While you are holding the frog captive, make some additional observations about its structure and its behavior. For example, does the frog keep its eyes open when it eats? How does it sit? Write a description of a sitting frog. How many vocal sacs does it have? Where are they located?

When you finish your observations, be sure to return the frog to where you found it.

Effects of Temperature on Frog Calls. Herpetologists have learned that air temperature determines when frogs will call as well as the rate at which the calls are made. In the northern cricket frog *(Acris crepitans)*, the call rate increases as the temperature increases. Similar results were noted in the advertisement call of the gray tree frog *(Hyla versicolor)* and in the release calls of several species of toads *(Bufo* spp.)

The chart below gives the range of air temperature at which certain frogs will call. Within this range the rate of the calls will change. The frog populations represented live in Louisiana, Georgia, Alabama, and Mississippi. How does the air temperature affect the rate of calling of frogs in your area?

Frogs are known to be sensitive to footfalls on the soil. They can quiet a

FROG CALLS

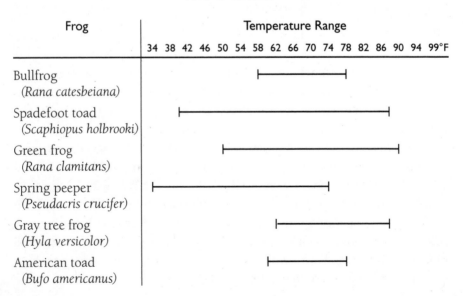

calling male many yards away. Try to sneak up on a calling frog. How close can you get to it before it stops calling?

Unsolved Mysteries. Although herpetologists have learned a great deal about frogs, there are still many mysteries to be solved. For example, how far do frogs travel from their winter shelters to reach their breeding pools? Do individual frogs go to the same pool each year to breed? Is this the same pool where they were hatched? How do the males identify the females of their species? Are frogs selective about where they lay their eggs? Where do they go and what do they do during the months that follow the breeding season? Perhaps you will have additional questions about frogs after you have spent some time observing them.

CHAPTER NOTES

1. Frog Calls. Calling is the most expensive activity in the life of an adult male frog in terms of the energy it requires. During the breeding season, male frogs call hundreds or thousands of times each night. The calling behavior of frogs can cost more than calories, as predators often use the calls to find tasty meals. The life of a frog is often the price a species pays for successful mating and the subsequent arrival of a new generation of frogs.

To produce calls, frogs take air into their lungs through their nostrils and pump the air rapidly back and forth from the lungs to a resonating chamber

three types of vocal sacs in frogs

single external
vocal pouch

paired pouches, swelling into
spheres above arm

single pouch, largely internal

called the vocal sac. In its journey the air passes over the vocal cords, causing them to vibrate and produce the familiar "croak." If you have ever tried to sleep near a frog pond, you know that croaking can continue throughout the night. When calling, a frog never needs to open its mouth.

2. Dip Nets. A good dip net has a long handle and a strong net bag with small mesh. The frame should be made of steel rather than aluminum, which is softer and tends to bend. You should be able to remove the frame so that you can replace torn bags as needed. Two suppliers: Carolina Biological Supply Co., Burlington, NC 27216; Wards Natural Science Establishment, Inc., PO Box 1712, Rochester, NY 14603.

3. Eyelids. Since frogs live both in water and on land, their eyes must be able to function both when exposed to air and when submerged. The biggest problem for an eye in open air is that it might dry up; to prevent this, frogs have thick eyelids. A thin, transparent fold called the nictitating membrane passes over the eye from bottom to top and serves to moisten and protect the eye by washing it with a thin film of tearlike liquid secreted by glands in the eye. This liquid contains lysozyme (an enzyme found in tears and in egg whites), which protects the eyes from bacteria, viruses, and fungi that sneak in under the eyelids.

Frogs cannot turn their heads as we do. To compensate for this lack of neck motion, frogs' bulging eyes provide them with a wide range of vision. This helps them find food and spot predators. You need only to sneak up on a frog to find out how well this design works. Frogs see well in twilight, and their night vision is extremely good. When frogs slip beneath the water's surface, the nictitating membrane rises to cover the eye. As tadpoles, their eyes are suited to life in the water. During this phase of their life, frog's eyes more closely resemble those of fish than those of adult frogs.

4. Camouflage. Frogs have lightly colored underparts that contrast sharply with their darker tops. This is called countershading and is part of the frog's camouflage. The light coloring along the underside of the frog makes it difficult for a deep-swimming predator looking toward the surface of the water to see its prey as it swims along the surface. It is equally difficult to see the dark upper surface of the frog against the dark background of the pond bottom when looking down through the water.

The mottled pattern found on frogs also serves to make the frog difficult to see because the irregular outline breaks up the form of the frog's body. When looking for frogs, your eyes see the disruptive pattern as part of the vegetation in the frog's habitat.

5. Eye Shine. In the dark, our pupils become large black circles. Their

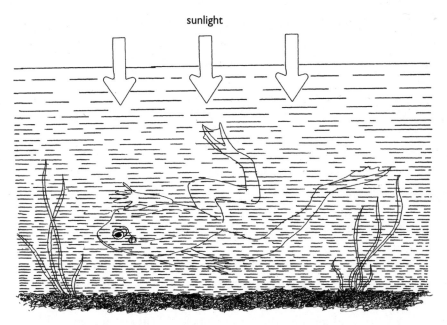

sunlight

Viewed through the water, the dark dorsal surface of the frog is difficult to see against the dark bottom of the pond.

size is controlled by the muscular irises, which contract as light diminishes. This process allows the maximum amount of available light to reach the rods of the retina; however, not all the light that passes through the pupil reaches the rods. Some of it is absorbed by surrounding tissues and is not available to illuminate our way in the dark.

Other critters have evolved different strategies for night vision. Owls, known for their nocturnal activity, have eyes that contain only rods, and their night vision is far superior to ours. The eyes of cats and water-bound dolphins contain many thousands more rods than our eyes do, and they see very well in the dark.

Another device developed by night-wandering animals is a layer of specialized cells called the *tapetum* that lies behind the retina. These mirrorlike cells reflect light back through the retina where it has a second chance to stimulate vision cells. You can see the tapetum when the eyes of skunks, raccoons, cats, and other animals are caught in the beam of light from a flashlight or the headlight of a car. Look for the red, yellow, or green eyeshine in our common night stalkers. You can learn to identify some animals by the color of their eyeshine.

6. Frog Eggs. The bullfrog (*Rana catesbeiana*) produces an enormous egg mass, two to four feet across. Each of the several thousand eggs is contained in a gelatinous envelope. The green frog (*Rana clamitans*) deposits 1,000 to 3,000 eggs in a surface film. Each egg is enclosed in two jellylike envelopes. The egg mass may be attached to vegetation or free floating. A spring peeper (*Pseudacris crucifer*) individually deposits 250 to 1,000 very small (two-mm.) eggs, which are generally attached to vegetation. The 2,000 eggs of a gray tree frog (*Hyla versicolor*) are laid in packets of 6 to 45 eggs each that float freely or are attached to vegetation. The American toad (*Bufo americanus*) deposits 4,000 to 8,000 eggs in long, double strands. Eastern wood frogs (*Rana sylvatica*) produce a mass of 1,000-plus eggs attached to submerged twigs or resting free on the bottom of the pond. Fowlers toad (*B. fowleri*) lays up to 8,000 eggs in strands in aquatic vegetation. The northern leopard frog (*Rana pipiens*) deposits 4,000 to 6,500 eggs in masses in shallow water, sometimes attached to twigs.

7. Tadpole Development. A newly hatched tadpole lacks a mouth. In some species the tadpole attaches itself by means of a sucker under its head, which you can see with the aid of a hand lens.

Behind the tadpole's head there are a pair of feathery growths, which are external gills. The tadpoles use these gills to remove dissolved oxygen from the water. Through the process of diffusion, dissolved oxygen passes into the tadpole's bloodstream and waste products such as carbon dioxide are removed. Water escapes from the tadpole's body through a tiny hole called a spiracle.

The main food for the tadpole is pond scum, consisting of algae (small plants) and bacteria. Included in the diet is the decaying plant material from the bottom of the pond.

Soon the tadpole will lose its gills and develop a set of lungs. You will know that the tadpole has become an air-breathing creature when you see it swim to the surface of the water and gulp for air.

Tadpoles have a sensory perception system called the *lateral line system,* composed of sense organs that appear as a series of light and dark dots. The line of dots form curving rows on top of the head and around the eyes and sometimes extend to the tail, making three irregular rows on each side of the tadpole. This system is similar to the lateral line system found in fish and allows the tadpoles to detect low-frequency vibrations, turbulence, and pressure changes such as those made by passing creatures or by ardent tadpole collectors wading through the pond. Vibrations from the tadpoles' watery environment are channeled to sensory receptors on the lateral line system. It is believed that this system is responsible for keeping schools of tadpoles together.

CHAPTER 6

Moths

WORLD-CLASS POLLINATORS

At day's end, darkness slowly covers the woodland floor and hides field and meadow. The azure sky of the summer day deepens to jet black. As bird songs cease, butterflies find refuge in tall grasses, and squirrels find safety in their treetop hideouts, night-flying moths begin to stir. The first group of these night fliers appears at twilight. As the night matures, different species of moths appear and begin the task of drinking nectar from flowers. The most moths are out around midnight. They slowly retreat during the night, until by dawn only a few moths linger for a last sip of nectar.

Moths belong to the insect order called Lepidoptera, which comes from the Greek words for "scale" (*lepido*) and "wing" (*ptera*). The moths' more flamboyant relatives, butterflies and skippers, also belong to this order. It may come as a surprise to many that there are about 10,000 species of moths in North America, about fourteen times the number of butterfly species. The adult moths we see dancing around a street lamp or fluttering from one flower to another in our gardens do not resemble the creatures that hatched from eggs weeks before. In fact, for most of their life cycle moths bear no resemblance to the adults that spawned them. These fascinating insects experience complete metamorphosis (from the Greek word for "change"). Moths begin their lives as eggs laid in clusters or singly on the vegetation of plants that will then be food for the hatchlings. When it leaves the egg, the moth is a tiny caterpillar called a larva, with a voracious appetite and mouthparts made for chewing and chomping. It is a virtual eating machine whose sole purpose is storing fat and protein—these nutrients must nourish not only the larva but also the moth that it will become. In its next stage as a pupa it will not eat at all, and as an adult moth it sips nectar for energy rather than for growth.

Like lobsters, barnacles, ants, and other arthropods, the caterpillar must shed its tough external skin from time to time to accommodate its growing body. A caterpillar will molt several times before entering the pupal phase.

Prior to becoming a pupa, many moth caterpillars build cocoons—tough, protective coverings made from silk, often incorporating bits and pieces of leaf litter. Each species of caterpillar makes its cocoon in a slightly different way: some are built on trees and shrubs; others simply lie on the forest floor. With some practice you can identify which type of moth will emerge from a particular cocoon. The winter, when trees and shrubs are without their leaves, is an ideal time to look for cocoons. Some of the moths that do not build cocoons pupate in crevices in the leaf litter on the forest floor or in cells they have built beneath the ground. The members of one

life cycle of a moth

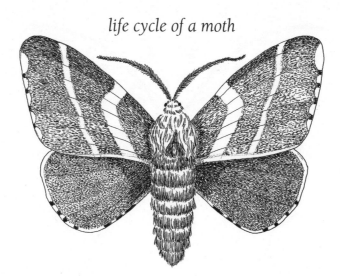

5. Like many adult moths, the eastern tent caterpillar moth (Malacosoma americanum) consumes no food and so has only a few days to mate and lay its eggs before it dies.

1. The female lays a band of eggs around a small twig and covers them with a foamy brown substance that hardens and protects the eggs over the winter.

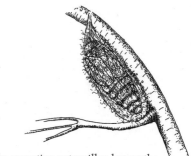

4. The pupating caterpillar leaves the tent and makes a thin creamy to pale yellow cocoon on or near the host plant. The pupa is often visible inside.

2. The larvae hatch in spring and form silky tents in the crotches of tree linbs.

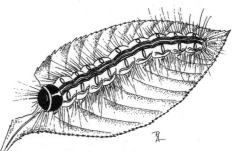

3. They feed outside their tents, using them only for resting. They grow by molting.

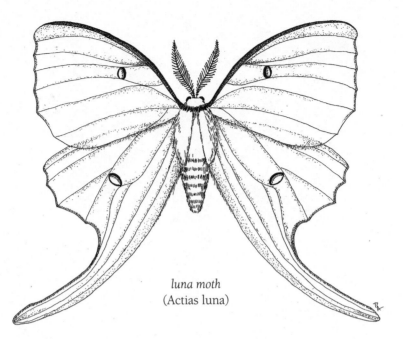

luna moth
(Actias luna)

family of moths, the sphinx, protect themselves during the pupal stage by becoming hardened after they have dug underground.

When in the pupal phase of life, the caterpillar may appear to be in a period of rest, but this is really a time of incredible change. All of the tissues that make up its body are broken down and re-formed. At the end of the pupal stage, which can last about twelve weeks, the caterpillar emerges as an adult moth complete with two pairs of wings, six legs, a hairy body, and a pair of antennae. This process requires a huge amount of energy, generated from the metabolism of nutrients stored during the larval stage. The adults of some species cannot eat because they lack mouthparts and other digestive organs. One such moth is the graceful luna moth, a member of the Saturniidae family, which lives just one short week. As adults, moths mate, lay eggs, and die. Some moths live longer than the luna and eat some nectar, which gives them energy for flying.

Adult moths rank with bees as world-class pollinators—an occupation that's a by-product of their eating habits. The moth is equipped with a long, strawlike tongue (proboscis) designed for sucking the sweet, sugary solution that flowers store within their nectaries. Almost any flower that produces nectar can be tapped by at least one species of moth or by their cousins, the butterflies; the length of the moth's proboscis coincides with the depth of the trumpet on the particular type of flower that nourishes it. There is an African orchid with a trumpet that stretches an incredible ten to thirteen inches, and the moth that feeds on it has a sipping straw that is the same enormous length. When a moth is not feeding, the sipping straw rests beneath its head, coiled like a watch spring.

That moths pollinate flowers is purely accidental, as they have no interest in pollen as food. Moths can't feed on protein-rich pollen granules because they lack the digestive enzymes necessary to reduce complex pollen grains into nutrients. When a moth reaches deep into the corolla of the flower for nectar, pollen grains stick to its hairy body. As the moth flits from flower to flower, it inadvertently carries the pollen from one flower to another, thus fertilizing them in a process called pollination. Since most moths are nocturnal, the flowers they pollinate display light, distinctive colors—usually pale yellow, pale pink, or white—that make them more visible in dim light. Flowers pollinated by daytime insects are usually darker.

One easily observable characteristic that moths and butterflies share is that their wings are covered with scales. Although you can't see individual scales without the aid of a powerful magnifier, they come in a variety of sizes and shapes. Some are square, some are round, and some are long and narrow. If you have ever handled a moth, you have probably noticed the slippery dust that remains on your fingertips after the moth gets away. This talclike material is made up of microscopic scales that easily slide off the wings, a quality that facilitates the moth's escape from tight places such as spiderwebs and also helps it to slide free of your grasp. Shedding a few scales is of little consequence to the moth, but if it loses enough of them in a struggle for free-

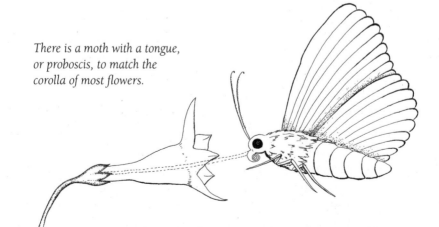

There is a moth with a tongue, or proboscis, to match the corolla of most flowers.

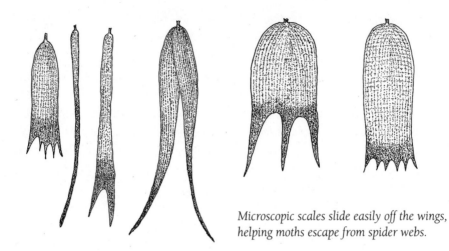

Microscopic scales slide easily off the wings, helping moths escape from spider webs.

dom, the moth can become unbalanced and unable to fly well—an easy meal for bats, birds, and other predators.

Each scale is so small that it takes tens of thousands of them to cover a little more than one-half square inch. If you were to look at the scales under a high-powered microscope, you would see a hollow structure much like the frame of a house with struts, posts, and a great deal of space. Incorporated into the structure are pigment granules, so if a moth lost all its scales, it would be colorless. Many of the soft earth tones worn by moths are due to melanin, pterdine, and other color-producing chemicals, by-products of metabolic activity during the pupal phase. Other colors are caused by the manipulation of light as it reflected, refracted, and scattered through the architecture of individual scale cells. Specific color patterns are unique to moth species. In smaller and more primitive moths, such as carpet moths and clothes moths, the colors are usually dull brown, buff, white, and gray, with an occasional shimmer of metallic bronze or black to add some zing to their otherwise drab coloration. In larger moths, such as hawkmoths and saturnids, the scales are often brilliantly colored in orange, yellow, or red and may form a variety of patterns on the wings.

Some patterns convey warnings to would-be attackers. For example, "eyespots" that resemble vertebrate eyes are worn by polyphemus moths. If one of these moths is threatened, it spreads its wings; the sudden exposure of these "eyes" triggers an escape response in predators such as small passerine birds. The eyespots seem to say, "Leave me alone, or you'll get it." Small eyespots on the wing margins of other moths convey similar messages. The wings of some moths provide camouflage while at rest because they resemble dried leaves, whereas other moths' wing patterns make them look like beetles, spiders, and other undesirable snacks. Some moths have brightly colored wings to divert predators' attention from vital organs. Whatever the pattern, it helps to keep hungry predators at bay.

The colors and patterns on moth wings are important for avoiding daytime predators, but they do not help in the mating process. Male and female moths encounter each other when they are active at night. In this they differ from butterflies. Moths have developed an elaborate mate-finding system that, independent of vision, involves the sense of smell.

In the activities section of this chapter, you will discover that moth wings are covered with scales. This is somewhat unusual in the insect world. Many butterflies also have scales on their wings, but the fact that some do not indicates that scales are not necessary for flight or for coloration. Scales seem to have evolved from hairs that covered the wings of the moth's ancestors, the aquatic caddisflies. But why did they evolve? Scientists once thought that the scales provided structural reinforcement, but a newer theory suggests that the scales help to prevent heat loss during the cooler nights.

Moths, like other insects, are cold blooded; their internal temperature is determined by the temperature of the environment. If a moth were to rest on a chilly night, it would have difficulty getting back into the air because it would have to use energy to warm itself before resuming flight. This takes

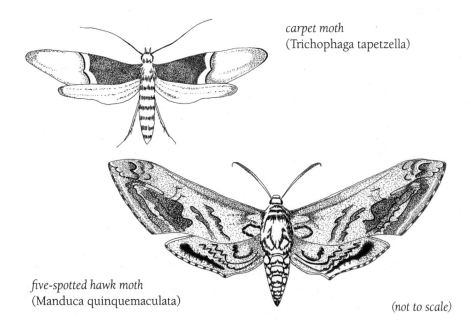

carpet moth
(Trichophaga tapetzella)

five-spotted hawk moth
(Manduca quinquemaculata)

(not to scale)

polyphemus moth
(Antheraea polyphemus)

valuable time from feeding and increases the moth's chance of becoming a meal for a hungry predator. You can observe a moth's warming-up process by capturing one in a collecting jar. Cover the jar with plastic wrap and puncture some holes in it. Put the jar in the refrigerator for several hours, and then remove the jar and watch the moth wake from its torpor. You will see its wings quiver; this is the warming process.

Like other creatures of the night, moths are often persecuted as a group because of the unacceptable behavior of a few. For example, only about two species, or 0.002 percent of the total moth population, are responsible for eating holes in our treasured woolens, and an additional small percentage of moths are agricultural pests. You may have met some of these in your garden—a member of the cutworm clan sharing an ear of corn with you or a codling moth larva housed deep inside a prized apple. But these are the exceptions rather than the rule in the moth world. Their role as pollinators and as food for many birds and bats far outweighs the damage done by a few species.

Moths come in an array of colors, shapes, and sizes. Some moths have robust, hairy bodies, whereas others sport sleek bodies with little hair. Some moths have elongated wings; others have rounded wings. Some moths are dressed in subdued earth tones that befit night fliers; others are clothed in more colorful garb such as the reds and oranges that we associate with their cousins the butterflies.

To help sort through this vast order of insects, moths have been conveniently divided into two groups: the microlepidopterans (small moths) and the macrolepidopterans (large moths). The notorious clothes moth is a small moth. Other small moths are responsible for plant galls, those swellings you often see on goldenrod stems and on the twigs of oak trees. As caterpillars, many micromoths make their homes on the broad leaves of trees and shrubs and in the terminal shoots of some North American pines. Others prefer a diet of some agricultural crops such as squash, grains, and tomatoes. Many micromoths have wing spans of less than one-half inch, or only a few millimeters.

The biggest of the macrolepidopterans is probably the atlas moth of India, Indonesia, and China, whose wings span twelve inches. You will have an opportunity to meet some of the larger moths in the activities section that follows.

After you have been moth watching for a while, you will discover the tremendous variety that exists among this fascinating group of insects. It is this quality that has made them so successful. After all, they have been swooping through the night sky for at least 150 million years.

The atlas moth (Attacus atlas) is the world's largest moth in overall size with a twelve-inch wingspan.

THE WORLD OF MOTHS

What to Bring	Science Skills
basic kit	*observing*
insect net	*communicating*
red or yellow cellophane	
white sheet	
gallon jar or fish tank	
dauntless spirit	

OBSERVATIONS

There are more than 10,000 moth species in North America. Those included in the activities that follow are the largest and most striking of our moths. They are representatives of the following families: sphinx or hawkmoths (Sphingidae), the giant silkworm moths (Saturniidae), the underwings (Arctiidae), the noctuids (Noctuidae), geometer moths (Geometridae), and the prominent moths (Notodontidae).

You will discover that moths come in a variety of sizes, shapes, colors, and patterns. You will also find out that every generalization made about moths and their families is accompanied by many exceptions.

How to Find Moths. Most moths are active from dusk to dawn. Even at night they are not hard to find because they gather around lighted street lamps and porch lights. To gather moths, hang a white sheet over the outside of a lighted window and turn off all other lights in the vicinity. Moths and other insects of the night will cling to your sheet. How many different kinds of moths do you attract? Do any of them seem to gather in a group? If so, separate them. Do they regroup? Why do you think they behave this way? (See Chapter Note 1 for information on pheromones.) Can you identify the female in your group of moths?

You can also hunt for moths in a garden using a flashlight whose beam is covered with red or yellow cellophane. As you shine the flashlight around the flowers you may spot the copper glint of moth eyes (from the Noctuidae family of moths) as the creatures feed on flowers.

Is It a Moth or a Butterfly? Capture a moth using the lighted-sheet method and an insect net or your hand. Because moths see motion and not color, sneak up from behind and move your cupped hand slowly for the capture. Once you have the moth, put it in a container with a lid and place the container in the refrigerator (not the freezer) for several hours or overnight. This will make the moth very sluggish. When you remove the chilled moth, you can observe it at your leisure. Of course, as the moth warms up, it will begin to move and will soon become as active as it was when you caught it.

Moths and butterflies share many similar characteristics, and this frequently makes it difficult to tell which is which. The following chart will help you decide which you have caught and chilled. After you make your observations, release the moth (or butterfly!).

Trait	Moth	Butterfly
Antennae or feelers	Hairlike or feathery	Slender with a club at tip
Body	Stout and furry	Smooth and slender
Wings	Elongated; when at rest lie flat like shingles on a roof; hook-and-bristle coupling keeps fore- and hind wing together in flight	Large relative to body weight; rounded; held vertically at rest
Flight	Stiff and erratic; a series of uninterrupted flaps; no gliding	Smoother and more graceful; a series of flaps followed by a glide

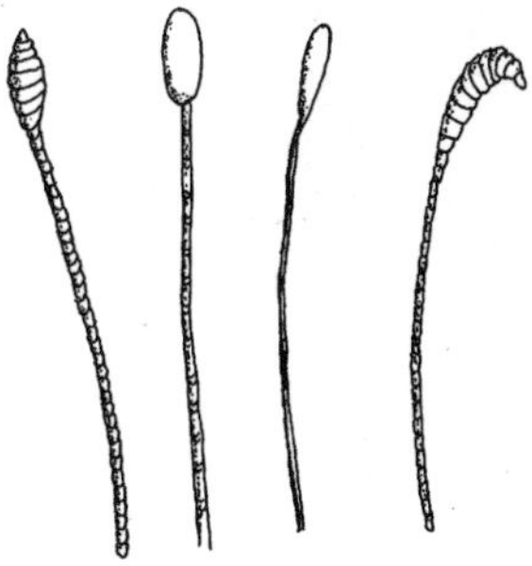

Insect antennae are densely covered with microscopic setae. They are used to touch, taste, and smell.

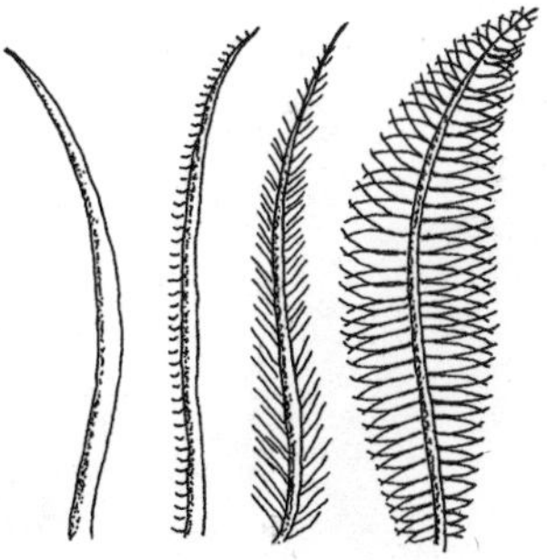

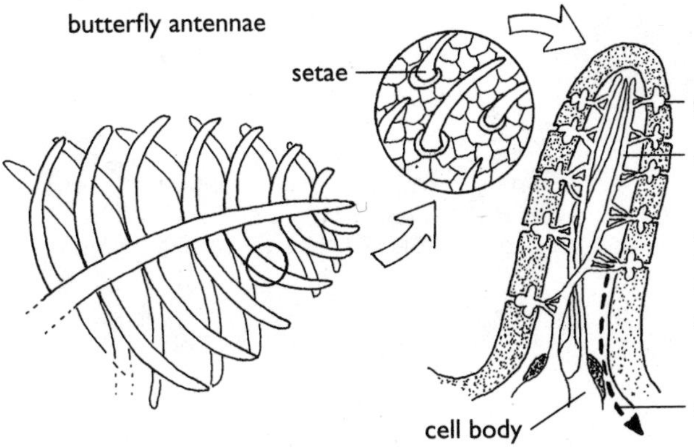

butterfly antennae

moth antennae

setae

pore

nerve fiber

This enlarged view of a setae shows how messages are passed to the central nervous system.

cell body

nerve impulse

When you are trying to decide whether you have captured a moth or a butterfly, the most reliable of these characteristics are the antennae or feelers. If the antennae lack the swelling or club at their tip, you have found a moth. (See Chapter Note 2.)

A Close-up of Moths. Capture a few moths and put them into bug boxes. Describe the shape of each body. Are they the same? Is the body of one moth hairier than another? Are some of the hairs gathered into clumps? Describe

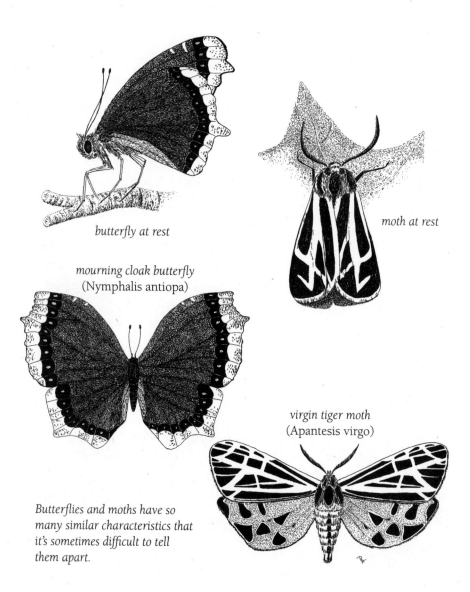

butterfly at rest

moth at rest

mourning cloak butterfly
(Nymphalis antiopa)

virgin tiger moth
(Apantesis virgo)

Butterflies and moths have so many similar characteristics that it's sometimes difficult to tell them apart.

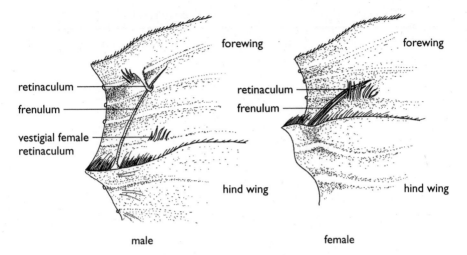

forewing

forewing

retinaculum

frenulum

vestigial female
retinaculum

retinaculum

frenulum

hind wing

hind wing

male

female

The two sets of wings are hooked together when a moth is in flight.

their colors. Is the body one color? If not, how are the colors patterned? Is the thorax (the part where the wings are attached) a different color than the abdomen? Which of the three types of antenna do your moths have? (See illustration.)

Moths have two sets of wings. The larger are the forewings, and when at rest these wings hide the two smaller hind wings. How does the size, shape, and pattern of a hind wing compare with that of a forewing? If your moths are fairly large and you have a strong magnifier, you can see the spine that hooks the wings together when the moth is in flight.

Moth Groups. Scientists have divided the moth population into two groups on the basis of size. The moths you will meet in these activities belong to the group called mega, or large, moths. They represent seven families, each characterized by a set of common traits.

When beginning to observe moths, look for such traits as size, wingspan, color, wing design, and hairiness of the body. Entomologists (students of insects) use additional features such as the number and pattern of veins on the wings, the length of the tongue (proboscis), the number and characteristics of spines and spurs on the legs, and characteristics of the external reproductive organs. The list below includes some of the megamoths found most frequently in North America. As you find moths, try to put them into one of these groups.

Group	Characteristics
Sphinx or hawkmoths (sphingids)	Stout body that tapers to a sharp point Narrow wings Swooping, hawklike flight (hawkmoths) Wingspan: 2.8 cm.–17 cm. Fast fliers Examples: hummingbird moth; clearwings; pink-spotted hawkmoth; five-spotted hawkmoth
Giant silk moths (saturniids)	Large, very hairy bodies Large, roundish wings that don't taper Very beautiful Wingspan: 3–15 cm. Examples: buck moth, Io moth, luna moth, polyphemus, promethea
Underwings or catocala (noctuids)	Rarely seen at rest because of camouflage Color pattern resembles tree bark Easy to recognize when captured Hind wings are all black or orange or red with black bands Eyes reflect light Wingspan of most: 2–4.5 cm. Examples: white underwing, copper underwing
Cutworms, armymoths (the remaining noctuids)	Some brightly colored Most gray to brown with complex patterns of lines and spots Hind wing design usually simpler than forewing Attracted to lights and bait Often called owlet moths because of the way eyes shine when a beam of light strikes them Examples: beet army worm, dingy cutworm (Noctuids are the largest family of moths)
Tiger moths (arctiids)	Generally light colors such as yellow, white, orange, or red Wingspan: 1.2–7 cm. Attracted to light Example: Isabella tiger moth

Group	Characteristics
Geometers (geometrids)	Most have thin bodies Broad wings Wingspan: 1–6 cm. Forewings and hind wings similar color Example: large maple spanworm moth
Prominents (notodontids)	Drab, brown to gray Attracted to light Wingspan: 2.3–6.2 cm. Hairy legs Example: variable oakleaf caterpillar

Moths That Break the Rule. Some moths are day fliers; you can find them wherever the flowers that nourish them grow. One of these day moths is the hummingbird clearwing moth *(Hemaris thysbe)*. As its name implies, it hovers as it feeds. The snowberry clearwing *(Hemaris diffinis)* also shows this behavior and is often mistaken for a bumblebee. If you see one you will notice that it does not sit on flower heads the way a bumblebee does. The white-lined sphinx *(Hyles lineata)* is another day flier. (See Chapter Note 3.)

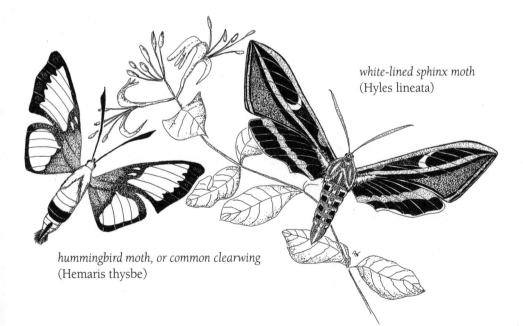

white-lined sphinx moth
(Hyles lineata)

hummingbird moth, or common clearwing
(Hemaris thysbe)

WHEN TO LOOK FOR DAY FLIERS

Moths	March	April	May	June	July	August	September	October	November
Virginia ctenucha (*Ctenucha virginica*), Arctiidae family			●————————————●						
The infant (*Archiearis infans*), Geometridae family	●————————————●								
Cecropia moth (*Hyalophora cecropia*), Sphingidae family			●————————●						
White-lined sphinx moth (*Hyles lineata*), Sphingidae family			●————————————————●						
Buck moth (*Hemileuca maia*), Saturniidae family							●————————————●		
Hummingbird clearwing (*Hemaris thysbe*), Sphingidae family		●————————————————————●							
Snowberry clearwing (*Hemaris diffinis*), Sphingidae family		●————————————————————●							
Slender clearwing (*Hemaris gracilis*), Sphingidae family			●————————————————●						

Some of these moths are called hawkmoths because their swooping flight resembles that of a hawk.

Moth Hangouts. Moths are known pollinators of night-blooming flowers, especially evening primrose, four-o'clocks, honeysuckle, and phlox. Spend some time with your flashlight observing your garden flowers or meadow wildflowers. Can you add any flowers to this list? (See chapter 2 for more on night-blooming flowers.)

Moth Records. During twilight and nightfall, look for moths feeding on wildflowers or on flowers in your backyard garden. If you get up very early on a few mornings, you might see the moths that feed at the crack of dawn. In your notebook make a record of your observations, including the date, the time, the weather conditions, and what the moth was doing. If you continue your observations for several seasons, you'll notice a relationship between the weather and moth activity.

WHEN TO LOOK FOR COMMON NIGHT-FLYING MOTHS

Moths	March	April	May	June	July	August	September	October	November
Polyphemus moths (*Antheraea polyphemus*), Saturniidae family			●———————●						
Salt marsh moth (*Estigmene acrea*), Arctiidae family			●—————————————●						
Isabella tiger moth (*Pyrrharctia isabella*), Arctiidae family		●———————————————————●							
Honey locust moth (*Sphingicampa bicolor*), Saturniidae family		●——————————————————————————●							
American dagger moth (*Acronicta americana*), Noctuidae family		●——————————————————————————●							
White underwing (*Catocala cerogama*), Noctuidae family					●————————————————●				
Pink-spotted hawkmoth (*Agrius cingulatus*), Sphingidae family				●——————————————————●					
Walnut sphinx moth (*Laothoe juglandis*), Sphingidae family			●———————————●						

Circadian Rhythms. Certain moths will appear at predictable times during the night. Below is a chart that will help you know when to expect certain moths to make their debut on the night stage.

- Late afternoon to twilight: prometheans (saturnids)—sphinx moths (Sphingidae family), *Hemaris* sp., pink-spotted hawkmoth (Sphingidae family), *Callosamia promethea* (Saturniidae family)

- Night: underwings (noctuids)—most species including tiger moths (arctiids), salt marsh moth, yellow bear *(Spilosoma virginica), Estigmene acrea,* Isabella tiger moth *(Pyrrharctia isabella), Catocala* sp.

- Dawn: sphinx moths (Sphingidae family), probably the same species as at twilight.

Moth Collections. Many naturalists preserve and mount collections of insects in glass-topped boxes. These collections can be of great value to scientists if careful records show when and where each insect was captured, and are often preserved in local museums for research purposes. Your local library should have books on how to preserve and mount insects.

Caterpillars. Even though caterpillars of various species of moths can look very different from each other, all caterpillars share certain characteristics. Below is a diagram of a "typical" caterpillar.

A Collection of Caterpillars. Summer and early fall are the most productive seasons to go caterpillar hunting. The illustrations below identify some of the characteristics of some common moth caterpillars and some of the food plants where you can expect to find them. Collect a few different caterpillars and make drawings or take close-up photographs of each. The chart below provides some clues that will help you in your search.

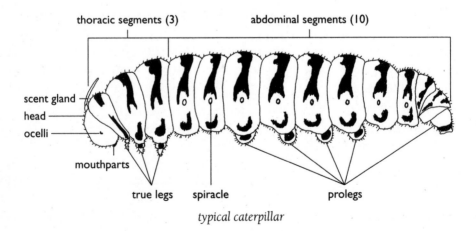

typical caterpillar

CATERPILLARS OF COMMON MOTHS

Body Features	Example	Food Plants
Smooth		
	White underwing	Poplar, quaking aspen, willows
Lumps and bumps	Giant silkworms	
	Cecropia	Silver maple, apple, poplar, oak, sassafras, gray birch, wild cherry
	Luna	Hickory, sweet gum, birch, oak, alder, beech, persimmon
	Promethea	Spicebush, wild cherry, sassafras
	Polyphemus	Oak, hickory, elm, maple, birch, linden, willow, chestnut
	Imperial	Oak, maple, linden, birch, elm
Hairy	Arctiids	
	Yellow bear	Rarely on trees; almost always on herbaceous plants, cabbage, corn, and other garden crops
	Virginia ctenucha	Grasses, sedges, irises
Bristles	Arctiids	
	Isabella tiger moth	Same as yellow bear; almost always on herbaceous plants such as clover, corn
	Salt marsh moth	Apple tree, corn, cabbage, cotton, peas, tobacco; mostly herbaceous plants, sometimes young trees

Body Features	Example	Food Plant
Branching spines	Saturniids	
	Io moth	Birch, clover, elm, maple, oak, willow
	Nevada buck moth	Alder, willow, poplar
Rear horn	Sphinx	
	Pink-spotted hawkmoth	Sweet potato and other members of the Convolvulaceae

Caterpillars that belong to the Geometridae family have a unique way of crawling, drawing the hind end up to the front end and causing a hump to form. They are often called inchworms.

Observing a Caterpillar. Capture several different kinds of caterpillars. Identify the tree or shrub where you found each one and describe the caterpillars' colors, structure, and other distinguishing features. How many legs does it have? On what segments do you find the prolegs (the stubby peglike appendages that help support the abdomen of caterpillar larvae when they are walking)? Some species of prominents lack the rearmost prolegs but hold the hind end erect. With the help of your hand lens, examine each side of a caterpillar's abdomen. Can you find tiny holes? On which segments are the holes found? What do you think these are for? (See Chapter Note 2.)

An Eating Machine. Watch a caterpillar eat its food. Does it pick at the leaf haphazardly, or is there a pattern to its eating? How long does it take to eat a leaf? How long do you think it would take a caterpillar to devour a small shrub with leaves approximately that size?

EXPLORATIONS

Keep a Caterpillar Diary. You can learn a lot about a caterpillar if you keep it in a gallon mayonnaise jar or an unused fish tank. If you found it while it was eating, be sure to keep a fresh supply of this food in the container with the caterpillar. If you found the caterpillar wandering about and not eating, it may be getting ready to enter the pupal phase of its life cycle and no food will be necessary. Be sure to put some twigs into the container so that if the caterpillar builds a silken cocoon it can use the twigs to support the structure. Don't forget to add some leaf litter, too, as the caterpillar may use some of it to spin into its cocoon.

If the caterpillar has not finished growing when you captured it, you may observe one of its molts. Record the changes you observe; does the caterpillar change color after a molt?

With the help of a hand lens, look at the caterpillar's mouth, jointed legs, prolegs, feelers, and eyes. Is it changing color? If so, it may be getting ready to become a pupa. Record the date of this color change. When does it begin spinning its cocoon? How does the caterpillar do it? What materials does it use? How long does it take to make the cocoon? Of course, you may have trapped a butterfly caterpillar. Wait and see.

The Effects of a Swinging Light on a Moth's Flight Path. Most people know that moths are attracted to a stationary light, but do moths respond in a similar way if the light is swinging? Find a place where you can sit comfortably for about twenty minutes. Swing a lighted flashlight back and forth with the beam of light pointing skyward. How do the moths behave? Explain their behavior.

Sugaring. Not all moths are attracted to light, but you can entice light-shy moths to your neighborhood with a technique called "sugaring." For this activity you will need to prepare a sweet and somewhat smelly brew. Mix a can of beer with one pound of dark sugar. Add one or two very ripe bananas, one-half cup molasses, one-half cup fruit juice, and one shot of rum. (This is not a highly developed scientific preparation. Nonacoholic beer will probably work just as well. Feel free to experiment with all kinds of variations.) Mix thoroughly. Pour into a large container and let it mellow outdoors for a few days. To keep the flies out of your concoction, lay a cloth over the top of the jar.

Next, saturate some dishwashing sponges with the potion and hang them from tree branches, fence posts, or posts you erect in your garden. (Moths will not come if your sponges are in open fields.) You could also smear the concoction on tree trunks with a paintbrush.

The best time to start "sugaring" is on a warm, still, starless night. Check your sponges frequently. If you want to examine the moths you attract, trap them in a container and use the "chill-and-check" method described earlier.

Moth Societies. For more information, you can contact the following organizations:

The Xerces Society, 10 S.W. Ash, Portland, OR 97204, phone (503) 222-2788.

The Lepidopterists' Society, 257 Common Street, Dedham, MA 02026.

CHAPTER NOTES

1. Pheromones are species-specific chemicals that female moths release when they are sexually mature. This moth perfume fills the night air and is picked up by males through their antennae. Although the night air becomes filled with these scents, we are unable to perceive them. As you might expect, male moths have slightly larger antennae than females.

2. Many moth species are equipped with sound-sensitive drums on their abdomens, with which they can pick up the sonar clicks of bats and evade them before becoming their next meal. These moths can hear vibrations between 15,000 and 60,000 cycles per second.

Moths have compound eyes, meaning that each eye is made up of hundreds of tiny, six-sided facets that fit together like the honeycomb of a bee. Each eye is equipped with a mirrorlike membrane behind the retina that reflects light back from the moth's eye into the night, producing eye shine. Some other creatures with eye shine are spiders, cats, dogs, and raccoons. Sometimes human eye shine is visible in photos taken with flash cameras.

Moth antennae, or feelers, are more or less hairy and end in a point. They are categorized as being like a comb, feather, or fuzzy thread. Antennae are essential because without them the moth becomes disoriented and loses its ability to fly. Moths also use their antennae to find their way to flowers and mates in the dark, as millions of odor-sensitive cells provide the moth with a map of the chemical highways that fill the night air.

Tiny holes on the sides of an insect's body are called spiracles. Air passes through these holes and enters a system of tubes called trachea. The number of spiracles varies with the species of insect, but most moths have nine pairs.

3. The moth family Sphingidae gets its common name, sphinx, from its larvae, which characteristically hold their bodies erect in a sphinxlike position. Most caterpillars that belong to this family carry a horn at the rear of the body.

THE PLAYERS

CHAPTER 7

Fireflies

FLASHES THAT COMMUNICATE

Fireflies are part of the warm memories I have of my childhood. On summer evenings my friends and I delighted in chasing the slow-flying blinking bugs of twilight. Before long a triumphant band of kids would return home with their captives safely jailed in jelly jars. I was particularly fond of fireflies and would keep them in a jar by my bed where I could enjoy their lights as I drifted into sleep. Then one afternoon a terrible thing happened: my mother accidentally released my bugs and I couldn't find a single one! It was a minor tragedy, so imagine my joy when, at nightfall, I saw the unmistakable syncopated blips of the fireflies in my room. They'd been there all along, camouflaged by daylight.

Fireflies are beetles, members of the insect order Coleoptera. The name of the order comes from the Greek word for "sheath" (koleon), which reflects the leathery quality of their outer wings. Like many other insects, beetles have two pairs of wings—forewings and hind wings—but beetles don't use their forewings (called elytra) for flying. In flight the beetles spread the elytra and use them for balance. When they are not flying, beetles use the elytra to cover and protect the delicate membranous flight wings.

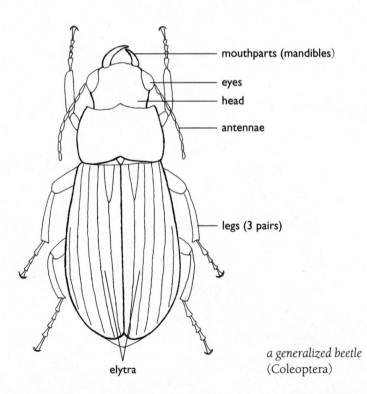

mouthparts (mandibles)

eyes

head

antennae

legs (3 pairs)

elytra

a generalized beetle
(Coleoptera)

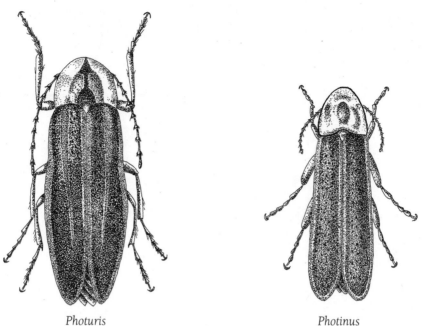

Photuris   *Photinus*

There are about 300,000 named species of beetles, but recent research in the canopies of tropical forests shows that there may be five or ten times that number. An estimated 2,000 of the named beetles are species of fireflies, which live in almost every earthly habitat. Although the great majority of fireflies thrive in the humid tropics, 200 species live in North America, and scientists tell us that new species are being discovered. Most of the fireflies we see belong to the genera *Photuris* and *Photinus* (also commonly seen is the day-flying, nonluminescent *Lucidota atra*). Winking lights from fireflies have delighted children and inspired poets, and scientists have learned some fascinating things about the nature of those lights and the role they play in the life of fireflies.

The cold light produced by fireflies is the result of a chemical reaction within the beetle's lamp. Located in the beetle's abdomen, the lamp is made up of several layers of cells. One of these layers houses large cells called photocytes, where the chemicals required for light production are stored. Another group of cells, called *reflector cells,* is specialized to intensify and direct the light. A network of air-conducting tubes and nerve fibers weaves an intricate web through the cell layers. A complicated chemical process involving oxygen, magnesium, luciferin, and the catalyst luciferase produces a tremendous amount of energy. We see this energy as light.

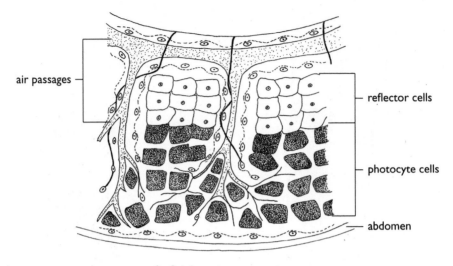

air passages

reflector cells

photocyte cells

abdomen

firefly's lamp in cross section

The conversion of chemical energy to light energy by the little beetles is about 98 percent efficient, which means that little waste in the form of heat is produced in the process. This is in sharp contrast to common incandescent light bulbs, in which only 3 percent of the energy is used for light. The remaining 97 percent of the energy becomes heat. Despite this efficiency, the light of a single firefly flash is not very bright. Someone figured out that if you wanted to convert your favorite incandescent lighting fixture to firefly light, you would have to trap about 25,000 fireflies and then train them to blink in a special sequence.

The cool light manufactured by living organisms through chemical action is called *bioluminescence,* and fireflies are not the only creatures that lay claim to it. Mushroom hunters tell tales of rotting logs that glow in the dark, but the cool light actually comes from bioluminescent fungi that grow on those rotting timbers. Nighttime beach strollers who see light flash in the wet sand with each footstep know that bioluminescent organisms live there. The greatest number of bioluminescent organisms live deep below the ocean's surface. Fireflies, however, are the only bioluminescent creatures that flash their lights.

Between 1910 and 1917 Frank McDermott began the difficult task of deciphering the codes that fireflies use to signal each other. In the 1960s scientists discovered that the story of firefly flashes includes mating rituals, cannibalism, and deceit. They learned that, in most species, a female firefly attracts the male with a series of rhythmic flashes unique to her species. Most females have wings and are capable of flight, contrary to the reputation given them by popular literature, but they prefer to flash from the ground or while perched on low-growing shrubs. The female's signal tells males where she is and that she is ready to mate. An interested male of the same species returns her signal, which the female recognizes and answers. Seeing her response, the male flies closer and repeats his flash. This two-way "conversation" continues until the male lands near the female and approaches her.

After they mate, the male flies off to find another receptive female. This simple-sounding procedure becomes complicated when several species of fireflies are flashing mating calls in the same area. Fireflies are able to avoid confusion because each species has a characteristic set of flash codes for each sex. Codes can differ among species in the following ways: flash length, interval length between flashes, flash pattern, flash rate, and time delay for females to answer. For example, a male *Photinus consimilis* emits a number of pulses ranging between two and four, four and nine, or four and eleven flashes for every two to six meters of horizontal flight. The female waits several seconds, then answers with double-pulsed flashes according to different patterns. The most efficient pattern would be a single flash with a single response signal, but no species seems to use it.

The color of their lights also helps fireflies to identify each other, although the exact function of the color remains unclear. Fireflies belonging

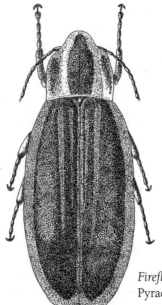

Fireflies in the genus Pyractomena *send out orange flashes.*

to the *Photuris* genus flash a green lamp, those of the *Photinus* genus flash yellow, and fireflies in the genus *Pyractomena* send out orange pulses. (See Chapter Note 2.)

Fireflies differ in habitat preferences as well. Some species prefer meadows and fields; others can be found in the margins separating fields from woods. Others fly languidly along watercourses or above suburban lawns. Additional differences are seen in the time of evening they emerge. Some fireflies begin sending messages just before sunset; others come out immediately after the sun goes down. Some fireflies flash for only twenty minutes each night; others can be seen flashing for several hours.

Despite these built-in separation techniques, some misidentification still occurs, and it is often intentional. Females in the genus *Photuris* can mimic the mating signals of females from other species and sometimes do this to lure unsuspecting males to their lairs and then eat them for dinner. This behavior is especially interesting because most adult fireflies do not eat, and those that do nibble on grass, sip nectar, or drink a few drops of dew.

For years scientists believed there were twelve species of cannibalistic fireflies, all in North America, but recent research indicates that members of some South American firefly genera make their living in this way, too.

Firefly flashes serve functions for reasons other than mating, as well. For example, a firefly may use its flashing lamp to illuminate a landing site, or a female might use her lamp to find a suitable place to lay her eggs. Humans also benefit from firefly light, as luciferase and luciferin are used in biomedical research that focuses on such problems as cancer, urinary tract infections, and water pollution. Additional studies indicate that luciferase may also help in our battle against malaria and tuberculosis.

THE WORLD OF FIREFLIES

What to Bring
basic kit
stopwatch
jar with lid
diligence

Science Skills
observing
comparing
measuring

OBSERVATIONS

Fireflies are excellent subjects for you to observe because you can do so without interfering with their lives. In the following activities, you will discover some of the coded language that fireflies use in their courtship rituals. Participation in the activities will not make you an expert, but you will discover that the world of this little beetle is very complex. You might even decide that you would like to go beyond this chapter and learn more about them.

Fireflies Emerge. Local weather conditions such as the amount of precipitation during the winter and early spring often determine when fireflies begin to emerge each spring from where they overwintered as larvae and pupae. Record the date of your first sighting and keep a record of the fireflies' arrival over a period of a few years. With the help of local newspapers you can find out if there is a relationship between the amount of snow and rainfall and the date of the annual appearance of fireflies in your neighborhood.

Some Early Observations. Where do the fireflies gather: in a field or meadow, by a stream, at the edge of a wooded area, over a suburban lawn? Do you see them high in the air near the treetops, or are they flying only a few feet above the ground? Describe the area. For how many weeks do they flash? What effect does the nightly weather have on their flashing?

A Close Look at Fireflies. With a sweep net or a swift and gentle hand, scoop up a few fireflies and put them in a clear container with a lid (a mayonnaise jar will do nicely). Punch some holes from the inside of the lid outward so that the fireflies don't scrape against the rough edges of the holes.

Find the two big insect eyes that are typical of many kinds of night fliers. How long are the antennae? Are they smooth or saw toothed? How many legs are there? Are they long or short? What does the length of the legs tell

The white circles and long blobs represent the flashes of several different species of fireflies. The arrows indicate the direction of their flight paths.

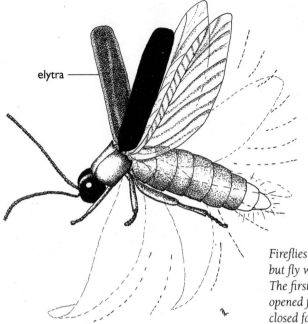

elytra

Fireflies have two pairs of wings but fly with only the second pair. The first pair, or elytra, are opened for balance in flight and closed for protection at rest.

you about the firefly's lifestyle? Look at the underside of the beetle. Describe the abdomen. Is it ivory or glazed looking or perhaps yellowish? On what segments are the lamps? Make a drawing of your firefly and keep it in your notebook.

Flash Patterns. The patterns of firefly flashes differ in a number of ways. With the help of a stopwatch and a friend, follow a firefly for several minutes. What can you find out about its flashes? How long is it between signals? On average, how far does the firefly travel between each signal? How long do signals last? Does the light produce a pattern? For example, the male *Photinus pyralis* scribes a "J" of yellow light against the dark backdrop of a summer evening. Look for this pattern.

Color of Flashes. Do you live in an area where there are yellow-flashing and green-flashing fireflies? You may notice that these two kinds of fireflies are active in different degrees of darkness. The fireflies that flash yellow lights are generally active during the early evening hours. Look for the twilight *Photinus* from sunset for about thirty minutes to the end of civil twilight (see Chapter 1). At this time their yellow lights will contrast with the green foliage of the surrounding trees and shrubs, making it easier for the fireflies to see one another. Fireflies with green lamps wait until it becomes darker before beginning to flash their mating codes.

Fireflies in Flight. Fireflies move slowly through the air, so it is easy to see how they use their forewings, or elytra, in flight. If you like to draw, make a sketch of your flying beetle; if you prefer, write a description of it. Look for the hind wings. Frequently when a beetle stops flying, the hind wings remain visible for a short time. What do these wings look like? Are they transparent or opaque?

When Do They Appear? At what time did you notice the first light of a firefly? What is the relationship between the onset of firefly flashes and sunset? When does the nightly display end?

Make the Light Stay On. One researcher thought he had found a new species of frog, only to learn that the frog had swallowed many fireflies. The light from the beetles was powerful enough to show through the frog's stomach and skin. Most fireflies in the northern temperate zone wink their lights unless they are in stressful situations. Capture one and hold it in your hand. Does it blink its light, or is there a steady glow from the firefly lamp?

Life Cycle. You are not likely to find the eggs, larvae, or pupae of many different kinds of fireflies, but you may see the larvae of *Photuris pennsylvanicus* walking on the ground in damp places, on roadsides, and on streambanks, with their lights intermittently glowing. The autumn is a good time to look for these creatures, which resemble trilobites. The diagram on the next page illustrates the very complex process of their development.

A large meal of fireflies can make a frog appear luminescent.

life cycle of a firefly

1. Female lays eggs on damp moss.

2. Larva hatches and grows by molting.

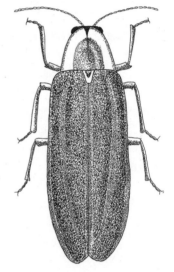

6. The metamorphosis is complete; an adult Pennsylvania firefly (Photuris pennsylvanicus) emerges from the chamber.

3. The following spring, larva burrows in soft soil.

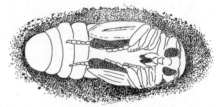

5. Pupa in the chamber (cutaway view).

4. Larva forms pupal chamber covered with body secretion that hardens into a waterproof coating.

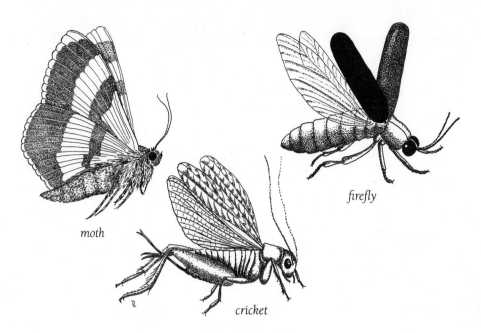

moth

firefly

cricket

EXPLORATIONS

Compare Wings. Capture a moth, a cricket, and a firefly. Put each into a separate see-through container (a bug box is a good choice). Compare the wings of your captives. Do they have scales? Are they opaque or transparent? How many pairs of wings does each insect have? How do these sets of wings differ? Where are the wings located? Look for the veins in the wings. The patterns formed by the veins are important characteristics that scientists use when they are trying to identify closely related species of insects. Make a drawing of each insect and its wings.

Colors of Firefly Light. Colors are good clues to identification. Keep a record of where you observed them.

Firefly	Time	Location
Photuris have green flashes		
Photinus have yellow flashes		
Pyractomena have orange flashes		

The Effects of Weather on Flashing. Observe fireflies on several nights. Record the temperature, cloud cover, moon phase, and humidity. What weather conditions seem to favor steady flashing of fireflies? (See Chapter Note 1.)

Date	Temp.	Humidity	Phase of Moon	Firefly Activity

Flight Altitudes. Different species of fireflies cruise at different heights above the ground. Some species hover just above the grass, some fly over our heads, and others fly just below the treetops. As you watch fireflies flashing from these different levels, do you notice different flash patterns?

Looking for a Mate. A male firefly signals from on high, using his large eyes to scan the night, which is alive with winking and blinking lights. Can you find a male and female pair signaling each other? Look for a signal from a male that seems to be homing in on a ground signal. Follow that male and see if you can find the responding female. Females are extremely difficult to locate, but you can sometimes find one by crawling around on a recently cut lawn.

Food Chain. Like the larval stage of other life-forms, firefly larvae are voracious carnivores. They feed on slugs, worms, snails, and other insect larvae that they have injected with poison from their jaws. The larvae have light organs on their abdomens but they differ from those of adults by giving off a pulsating glow rather than flashing. Do you think scientists are correct in suggesting that these lights warn predators to stay away from these foul-tasting creatures?

male signal

female response

CHAPTER NOTES

1. Temperature and Fireflies. Fireflies are seen in the stillness of damp, moonless nights, and rarely seen on cool breezy evenings. They will fly when temperatures are within the tolerable range between fifty degrees F and ninety degrees F. Those fireflies living in the north cannot fire their engines at temperatures below fifty degrees, whereas those fireflies that live in the southern part of the United States have adjusted to higher temperatures and usually cannot operate below fifty-seven degrees F.

2. Firefly Flashes. The descriptions of firefly flashes generally found in popular literature are initial descriptions that need work and refinement. You may be frustrated if you try to see the patterns described there. Firefly species and their flash patterns vary geographically and vary greatly with temperature.

CHAPTER 8

Bats

ALLIES IN THE INSECT WAR

As you watch a long summer day end, a brilliant red glow floods the western sky. Soon the light of the aging day grows dim and the blackness of night begins to creep across the land. The throbbing notes of the cricket orchestra swell from the ground into the night air. Soon you become aware of small, dark shapes looping, somersaulting, and fluttering above your head. Perhaps your first thought is that these darting silhouettes are evening birds such as whippoorwills or nighthawks, but you soon realize that those nimble fliers are actually bats, the precision hunters that snatch insects one by one from the night air.

Like other nighttime creatures, bats are subject to superstition. We associate them with nefarious activities, the evil Count Dracula, ghosts, and other mysterious and harmful creatures of the night. The fear is evident as you listen to the questions that arise whenever bats appear: Are they dangerous? Do they bite people? Do they suck blood? Do they get caught in people's hair? Do they carry rabies or other diseases? Our negative attitudes toward bats probably developed because many features of the bat's life are shrouded in mystery. There's a lot we don't know about bats, but we do know that these wonderful flying mammals are not a danger to us. Perhaps a closer look at bats and their behaviors will shatter some false notions that you may have and help dispel your unnecessary fears.

The early history of bats is found in ancient rocks where scientists have found the fossilized skeletons of the first bats to appear on earth. Although this record is incomplete, scientists know that bats have been choreographing their dances in the night sky for about 75 million years. It is suspected that bats originated in the early Paleocene or mid- to late Cretaceous. If this is correct, bats would have been whirring around in the sky when the dinosaurs roamed the earth, when flowering plants were just beginning their reign over the land. The foliage of the broad-leaved trees provided daytime shelter, and the pollen, nectar, and fruit supplied food for the vegetarian bats. Other bats took to the night sky to feed on insects. This adaptation to hunting at night permitted insectivorous bats to avoid competition with birds that hunted insects by day.

When you look at a bat, you are probably reminded of a mouse, but if you examine a bat carefully, you'll see five toes on each of its hind feet. Mice have only four toes on their hind feet. Possession of five toes is a characteristic that bats share with an animal called a shrew. Using this clue and other indications, most evolutionary biologists believe that bats share a common ancestor—a shrewlike animal that lived in the trees. Other scientists speculate that large, fruit-eating bats did not evolve from a shrewlike animal but from an ancestral primate. These scientists have found that visual pathways in the brains of large bats (megabats) such as the flying fox bat are similar to those found in primates. An analysis of gene structure also supports the primate-bat relationship. If this is true, then these bats may actually be thought of as flying monkeys. As primates ourselves, we humans find a special fascination with other primates and with the idea that at least some of our "close relatives" took up flying. These findings bring scientists into the age-old debate about whether similarities or differences are more important when assigning an animal to a particular group or phylum. Conflicts such as this are a natural part of scientific inquiry. You can read more about this fascinating dispute in the articles by Bailey and Gibbons that are listed in the Bibliography.

There is no dispute among scientists, however, about the fact that bats are mammals. They have body hair and mammary glands and give birth to live young, but unlike any other mammal, bats can fly. Their "hand" and forearm bones are similar to those found in other mammals but they are adapted to accommodate the bat's continuous wing membranes. This thin, double layer of skin encloses its somewhat elongated forearm; long, tapered fingers; and hind limbs. In some bat species, the tail is also enclosed by this membrane. A bat's fingers have great dexterity, so they can manipulate the wings to form umbrella shapes that trap insects, as well as hover in midair like hum-

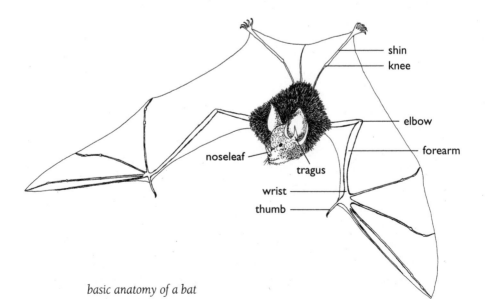

basic anatomy of a bat

Indian Ocean Island flying foxes are the largest bats, with a wingspan up to 5.6 feet.

mingbirds. In all species of bats, the clawlike thumbs of their extraordinary hands remain free outside the wing. Bats use this fine tool for clinging to the walls of caves, hanging from tree branches, and manipulating food and other objects. The wings are designed so that a bat can fold them close along its side like a collapsed umbrella. This feature lets the bat crawl along a flat surface without getting tangled in folds of skin.

Bats belong to the order Chiroptera, which comes from the Greek word *chiro,* meaning "hand," and *petra,* meaning "wing," references to the unique structure of the "hand-wing." Bats come in a variety of sizes and colors including dark brown, orange, yellow-gray, black, red, gray, and white. Bats have adapted to such a variety of climates that you can find them anywhere in the world except in the polar regions. A few red bats (*Lasiurus borealis*) have been found as far north as Southampton Island in the Canadian Arctic, but most species of bats live in the tropics because food is available there year-round.

The order Chiroptera is divided into two groups: large bats, or megabats (Megachiroptera), and small bats, or microbats (Microchiroptera). Megabats, often called flying foxes because of their foxlike faces, live in the tropics of Africa, Australia, and Asia and have wingspans up to six feet. Unlike their smaller relatives, many megabats are active during daylight hours and have large eyes and good vision. This feature, coupled with their finely tuned sense of smell, leads them to nutrient-rich flowers and ripe fruits, the staples of their diet. Their pointed, doglike snouts and long tongues allow them to reach into flowers for protein-rich pollen and sweet nectar, pollinating the flowers in the process. Some bats also help propagate tropical plants by eating their fruit and later depositing the seeds some distance from the parent. Bats in some regions of the world feed on fish, lizards, and mice, and the vampire bat that lives in the tropics eats the blood of cattle. This preference for blood has led the bat to occasionally inflict a pinprick wound in humans and has contributed to the superstition that all bats drink blood.

The smallest microbat is the bumblebee bat of Thailand, which weighs less than an average paper clip. All of the bats that live in the United States and Canada are microbats. These bats spend the day in dark places and hunt for food—usually flying insects—at night. Filling this nighttime niche permits them to be active when most predatory animals are at rest. Microbats do not see well in dim light, but their well-designed sonar systems more than compensate for that deficit. With this tracking capability, called echolocation, a bat can determine the size and shape of an object, how far away it is, and whether it is moving. To do this, the bat emits a stream of high-pitched clicks and squeaks that are inaudible to humans. When the sound waves hit an obstacle, they are returned to the bat as an echo. The bat "reads" the echo and acts accordingly. You can observe this sonar system at work if you watch a bat rapidly fly through a grove of trees. It never hits a single branch or twig as it pursues its next meal. The sending of the pulses and their return as echoes happens in a fraction of a second. We can hear sounds that are within the range of 20 to 20,000 cycles per second, or hertz. The pulses produced by bats are above 20,000 Hz (also expressed as 20 kilohertz or 20 KHz).

Only microbats echolocate by producing the high-frequency tones in the larynx. Some echolocation calls, such as those of the North American

Kitti's hognose (bumblebee) bat is the world's smallest mammal, about the size of a large bumblebee.

By means of echolocation, bats can find prey even on very dark nights.

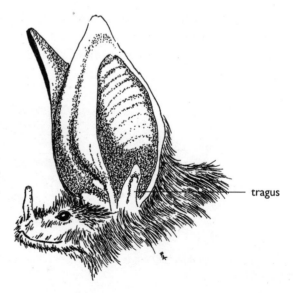

California leafnose bat
(Macrotus californicus)

tragus

Nyctinomoas, are audible to humans, but most of the gentle squeaks we hear are not the vibrations of the tracking system but communication among the bats. One species of macrobat produces high-frequency calls with its tongue, a more primitive form of echolocation than the laryngeal technique of the microbats. Leafnose bats, of which four species live in North America, release sound from megaphone-shaped mouths or queer-looking folds of skin on their noses.

Most microbats have a spearlike growth called the *tragus* that stands upright inside each ear. The tragus is somehow part of the echolocation system, but scientists have yet to discover its exact function. Ridges inside the fleshy part of the bat's ear are also part of the sonar system. Echolocation is an advanced strategy for navigating and hunting in the dark shared by dolphins, whales, some shrews, and a few species of South American birds.

Throughout the warm months of spring and summer, insect populations explode. As the numbers of these pests increase, so do the numbers of elec-

The little brown bat (Myotis lucifugus) *is one of America's most abundant bats.*

tric bug zappers in suburban neighborhoods. This human invention can't equal the work of bats, however. Scientists have estimated that a little brown bat (Myotis lucifugus) eats at least one-third of its body weight in insects in a half hour of foraging. At this rate, a population of Mexican freetail bats in Texas would eat 12,000 tons of insects per night. The insect diet of North American bats makes them our most important allies in insect control.

As summer fades into autumn, the supply of insects begins to dwindle and the nights grow cool. Soon freezing temperatures will cover the ponds with ice and the land will be in winter's grip. So in July, some species of micro-bats begin migrating to the warmer latitudes of Central and South America. By August, most migratory bats are on the move. Some species of bats that spend the summer in Canada and the northern United States migrate to certain areas of the American South to hibernate. The Mexican freetail bats migrate to Mexico and Central America, where they remain active.

Among hibernating bat species, scientists have discovered that wherever bats choose to hibernate, the temperature in the hibernaculum, or winter shelter, remains a few degrees above freezing. During the several months of hibernation, the bats' metabolism slows and their body temperature falls from 104 degrees F to approximate that of the surrounding air, about 40 degrees. If the temperature in the hibernaculum deviates from this optimum level, the bats respond by increasing their metabolism. There is danger in both falling and rising temperatures because in either case the bats draw excessively on their fat reserves and reduce their chance of surviving the rest of the winter. Should you find a hibernating bat, do not disturb it, or you may cause it to lose from ten to thirty days of fat reserves.

Most hibernacula contain only female bats and will become nursery colonies after the pups are born. The males of many bat species find other places to spend the winter, alone. The mortality rate for these male loners is usually quite high, but the isolation of adult males means the females have less competition for food. This aids the survival of the species because it increases the chances that a greater number of young will survive to reproduce.

During the warmer months, many bats use their winter hibernation caves as daytime roosts. They leave these roots at dusk to feed on night-flying insects and to drink by skimming water surfaces while flying. A colony of Mexican freetail bats leaving a cave often looks like a huge, black cloud; observers frequently compare the emerging bats to the whirling spiral of a tornado. Other bat species are solitary and may roost in tree hollows or hang upside down from branches. Bats in this position often resemble dead leaves or are camouflaged by the foliage. Solitary bats sometimes find the space

A young Mexican freetail bat (Tadarida brasiliensis) *is carried by its mother.*

behind window shutters or under loose tree bark to their liking. They look for a snug spot that is secluded and dark.

Bats mate in the fall, but the sperm remain inactive within the body of the female until spring, when fertilization takes place. A typical female bat will have one pup, but some bat species such as the silver-haired bat (*Lasionycteris noctivagans*) occasionally produce twins. The red bat (*Lasiurus borealis*) has been known to give birth to quadruplets. At birth the pups are relatively large, weighing about one-tenth of an ounce—one-fifth to one-quarter the weight of the mother. (This is like a 120-pound woman giving birth to a 30-pound baby!) Newborn bat pups are naked and begin suckling immediately. As long as their mothers can carry them, the pups cling to the mothers' mammary glands and accompany them on their nocturnal sorties in search of insects.

Most insect-eating bats pursue one prey at a time, unlike the nighthawks that seine the air with open beaks. Bats will eat whatever insects are available, including mosquitoes, moths, crickets, grasshoppers, midges, muffles, caddisflies, beetles, hoppers, and aphids. Little brown bats (*Myotis lucifugus*), which weigh about 8.2 grams (eight average paper clips), swallow an average of 1 gram of insects, or 1,200 fruit flies, per hour. Big brown bats (*Eptesicus fuscus*) weighing about 18 grams can gobble up 4 grams of insects in about an hour and a half.

In addition to eating insect pests, bats help humans in other ways. Bat colonies build up large quantities of guano, a nitrogen-based waste product that supports populations of unusual bacteria. Researchers have discovered that some of these bacteria produce enzymes effective in removing ammonia from industrial waste before it is released into ponds and streams. Because bat wings are nearly transparent, medical researchers have been able to study the effects of vaccines on bacteria by observing the blood as it flows through

big brown bat
(Eptesicus fuscus)

the network of veins in a bat's wing. They have also used bats to study the effects of hibernation on the aging process, and research on vampire bats contributes to the development of new and different anticoagulants for cardiac patients. Our friends the bats are also helping us to find new strategies that will help the blind become more independent.

THE WORLD OF BATS

What to Bring	Science Skills
basic kit	*observing*
a little courage	*recording*

Bats are not dangerous, but when you find one leave it alone. Your touch might startle it and it may respond like any other frightened animal by snarling, biting, and scratching. Scientists who study bats usually wear heavy work gloves when handling bats.

OBSERVATIONS

Where to Find Bats. Except for the nectar-drinking, pollen-eating long-nosed bats (*Leptonycteris*) of the southwestern United States, which forage during the day, most North American bats wait until twilight to begin hunting for insects. Although large roosts are easier to find than small ones, locating any of these daytime hangouts can be very difficult. Some species of bats gather in rock crevices where they are protected from the burning rays of the summer sun. Others snuggle in the crannies of bell towers or attics, and still others prefer to dangle from barn rafters. Sometimes bats like to recuperate from a night of hunting in the close spaces behind window shutters. The big brown bat *(Eptesicus fuscus),* also known as the house bat, is especially fond of shelter.

Bats that roost in churches, houses, barns, and other buildings generally give away their presence by a brown stain caused by their droppings running down the side of the building. Another sign of bats is the whitish guano that collects on the ground below a roost. If you are a patient and persistent observer, you may discover some bat roosts in your community. Another good way to locate bats is to ask a naturalist at a nature center about local bat populations. Some of the North American bats that prefer group living and congregate in buildings are the evening bat *(Nycticeius humeralis),* the big brown

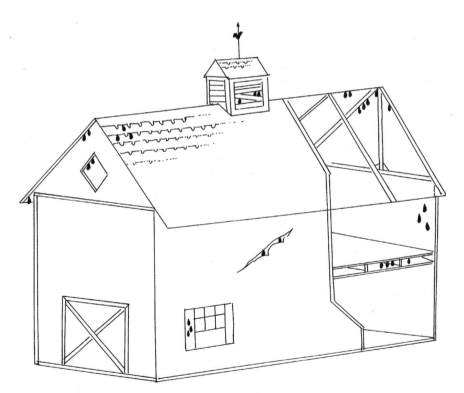

Some of the places to look for bats in barns and other buildings are illustrated in the diagram above.

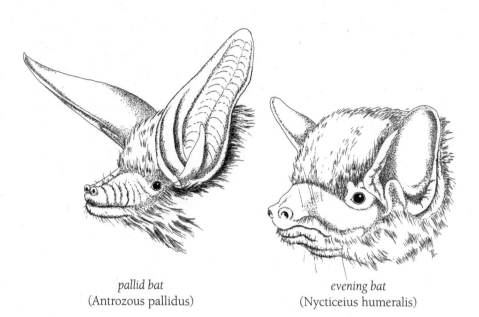

pallid bat
(Antrozous pallidus)

evening bat
(Nycticeius humeralis)

bat, the little brown bat, and the pallid bat (*Antrozous pallidus*). Although the Mexican freetail bat (*Tadarida brasiliensis*) gathers in huge colonies, it prefers to assemble in caves rather than in buildings.

Communal living is not for all bats. Some bats shun both buildings and caves and seek the solitude offered by a hollow tree, or simply hang from tree branches. Asleep in the cool shadows of the foliage, these bats usually go unnoticed because they resemble dead leaves. Young bats, still hugging their mothers, also find safety in trees. Hunting for solitary bats can exhaust the patience of the most skilled field worker. The eastern pipistrel (*Pipistrellus subflavus*), the most abundant bat in the eastern United States, prefers to roost in sycamore trees, but they're extremely difficult to find. The red bat, the silver-haired bat, and the hoary bat (*Lasiurus cinereus*) also like to hide in trees and shrubs.

Many people who live in or visit the southwestern United States know that millions of Mexican freetail bats roost in the caves of Texas and New Mexico, where they are featured as a tourist attraction. Unlike most bats that live in the eastern part of the United States, western bats generally roost in caves and deserted mines.

Listed below are some of the bats you are likely to find in and around your community. Although these are the bats we see most often, little is known about their habits and their haunts.

Little brown bats: Widely distributed across the United States and

Canada, this is our most abundant bat, often found with the big brown bat. Look for it in buildings, behind shingles or siding, or in attics.

Big brown bats: These bats range from Alaska and Canada south through the United States into Mexico. Their roosts include attics, barns, and other buildings; behind window shutters; in expansion joints beneath bridges; and occasionally in tree hollows. These bats hang around with the mouse-eared bats such as the little brown bat and its western cousin Yuma myotis (*Myotis yumanensis*). You also can find it with the Mexican freetail bat, with the pallid bat, and in close association with people

Evening bat: Found from Pennsylvania south to the Gulf Coast, this bat avoids caves but prefers buildings, where large nursing colonies are often

silver-haired bat
(Lasionycteris noctivagans)

red bat
(Lasiurus borealis)

eastern pipistrel
(Pipistrellus subflavus)

hoary bat
(Lasiurus cinereus)

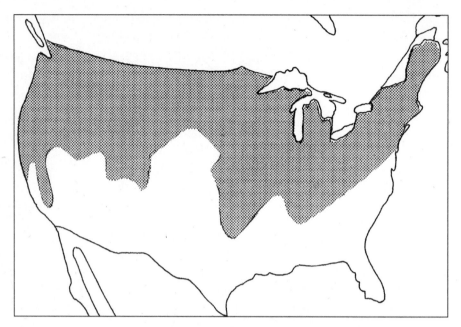

The little brown bat, widely distributed across the United States, is our most abundant bat.

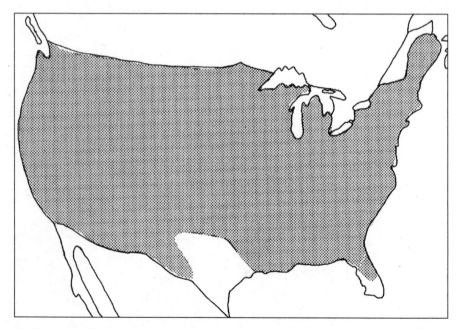

The big brown bat, which ranges widely throughout the United States, is found in close association with other bats and with people.

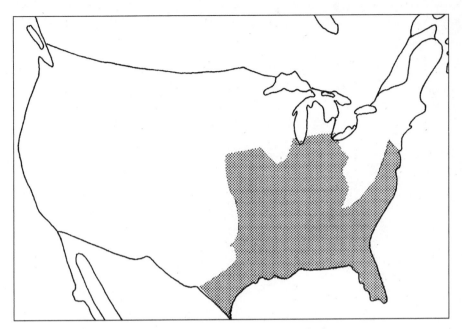

The evening bat is found from Pennsylvania south to the Gulf Coast.

found. Smaller groups of these bats will roost behind tree bark or in tree hollows. It commonly roosts with the Mexican freetail bat.

Mexican freetail bats: On the West Coast and in the Southeast, this bat prefers to roost in buildings. In Texas, Arizona, Oklahoma, and New Mexico, however, its preference for caves is well known by visitors and locals. Because these bats have been studied so extensively, we probably know more about them than any other kind of bat. They share buildings in the West with the pallid bat, the big brown bat, and the Yuma myotis. In the Southeast you can find them with the southeastern myotis (*Myotis austroriparius*) and the evening bat.

Pallid bat: These desert bats of the Southwest prefer rocky ledges and outcroppings where scrub vegetation such as mesquite grows. They are also found in Oregon and Washington, and a few colonies flourish in southern Kansas and Oklahoma.

The remaining bats prefer to spend the day in trees, and because of their solitary nature, they are extremely difficult to find.

Hoary bat: The most widespread of North American bats, the hoary bat is not yet found in Alaska. Its capture in the mist nets of bat banders suggests that there may be more of these rare bats than previously thought. This bat spends its days hidden in tree foliage, where it can be well concealed from

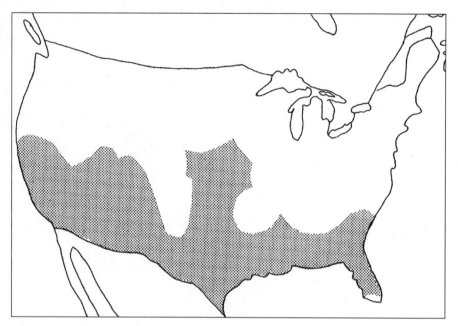

The extensively studied Mexican freetail bat ranges across the southern United States.

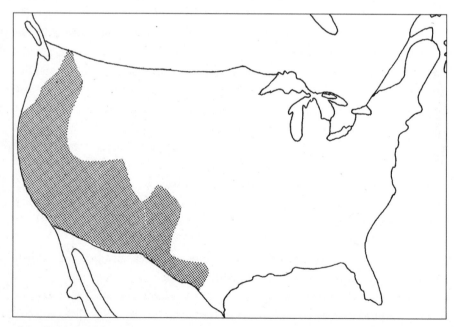

The pallid bat is found across the Southwest north to Washington.

above but have enough open space in the foliage below that it can drop down and begin its flight.

Red bat: Ranging from southern Canada and the eastern United States into Mexico and Central America, this tree-roosting bat prefers to hide beneath the leaves of sycamore trees, although the lush foliage of any broad-leaved tree will suffice. Infrequently they dangle like dead leaves from a branch or twig. Female bats roost with their young.

Silver-haired bat: Found primarily in the North but appearing in all states except Florida, these bats spend their days roosting behind loose tree bark or in abandoned woodpecker holes or bird nests. Sometimes they find solitude in outbuildings such as tool sheds and garages. Infrequently they have been found in small nursing groups.

What to Do When You Find a Bat. Although the roosting and hibernating places of many bats are still unknown, you can expect to find some bats if you look in the right places. When you find a bat, record the exact location of the roost in your notebook. What is the bat doing? Is it sleeping or cleaning itself? Is it hanging from a support, or is it lying flat on a building beam or on a rock surface? Is it roosting alone? Have you found a small group with

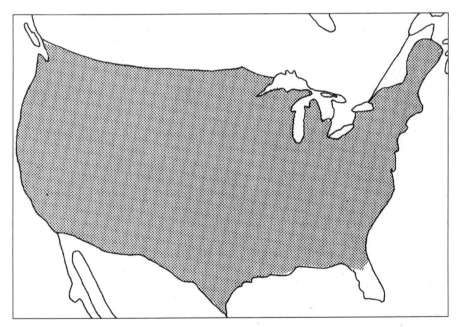

The hoary bat is the most widespread of North American bats but it is not yet found in Alaska.

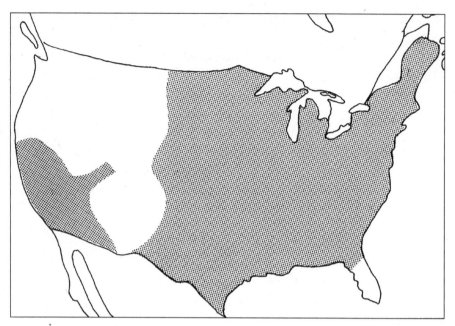

In the United States, the tree-roosting red bat ranges widely throughout the East.

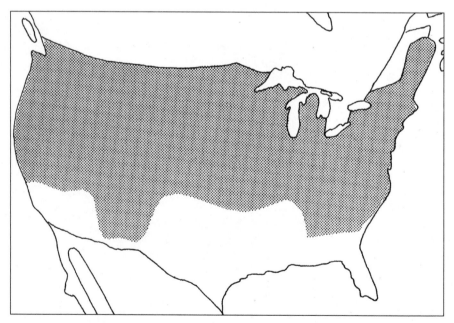

The silver-haired bat is found primarily in the North but appears at least occasionally in all states except Florida.

several dozen members, or is it a larger colony with hundreds or thousands of bats? If other bats are present in the roost, are they hanging in clusters? How many are in each cluster? Are the bats touching each other, or are they spaced some distance apart? (See Chapter Note 1.)

Bat Hygiene. Despite their smelly surroundings, bats are scrupulously clean, and their grooming process is quite orderly. A bat usually begins by washing its face with the front of its wing. If it's a leafnose bat, it uses its claws to scrape clean the nose-leaf part of its echolocation system. The ritual continues as a hind foot scratches its head and cleans its ears. A few licks to that foot cleans it. As the bat cleans its wings, the wing membrane stretches and recoils, as if the wing were made of elastic or spandex rather than skin. Finally, the bat attends to its fur with lips and tongue in much the same way as a cat cleans itself. If you find a bat without clean, fluffy fur, it is probably sick. Bats never defecate or void on themselves or each other despite the close quarters in a large colony.

A Close Look. If you find a bat during the day while it is resting, you probably can get a good look at it.

Wings. Observe the wings. Are they folded against the bat's body? Are they wrinkled or smooth? Find the fingers that make up the wing. How many are there? Where is the bat's claw, or "thumb," in relation to its other fingers? How do the hind legs support the wing? Look for the tail. What is its relationship to the membrane that extends between the bat's hind legs? Does the tail protrude beyond the membrane?

Head. Describe the bat's head. Does it look like a mouse or a little dog?

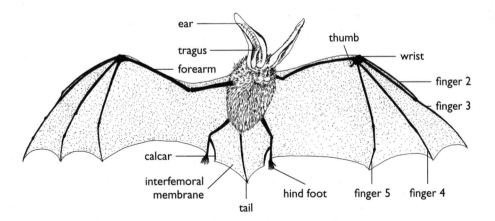

western big-eared bat (Plecotus townsendi)

Does it have a pug nose? Is there an odd flap of skin around its nose (a nose leaf)?

Mouth. Is its mouth shaped like a megaphone, a characteristic shared by bats that emit sonar clicks from their mouths? Look for the bat's incisor teeth. Describe them. What do they tell you about its diet? (See Chapter Note 3.)

Ears. Describe the bat's ears. Do they resemble the ears of a mouse? If so, you may have found one of the myotis bats (little brown bat, Yuma myotis, Mississippi myotis, or cave bat). If the ears are large and prominent, you may have discovered one of the big-eared bats (the pallid bat or the spotted bat). Is there a small, spearlike structure (tragus) at base of the outer ear? The tragus may function as part of the bat's sonar system.

Bats on the Wing. Although an occasional bat can be found flying about during the day, most bats take to the sky during the twilight hours. On a summer evening you can observe them in a dance of twists, spirals, and loops that is choreographed by the insects they pursue. Although it's difficult to identify a flying bat, the following are some points to keep in mind as you make your observations.

Describe its flight path. Is it straight and steady? Is it circular? Describe the habitat. Is there water nearby? Is the bat flying over a pasture? Was it flying close to the treetops? Did the bat spend most of its flying time higher or lower than the trees? Was it flying over a lawn or around lampposts? Was it alone, or were other bats flying nearby?

The following focuses on the flight pattern, wingspans, flight patterns, and foraging habits of the bats you will most likely see. Keep a record of bat sightings. Don't forget to include the date and time of your observations in your field notebook.

Little brown bat: A medium-sized bat with a wingspan of about eight inches (222–269 mm.), this mouse-eared bats prefers to forage over water, but if none is available it will hunt for food over pastures and lawns and among trees. They fly their zigzag flight ten to twenty feet above the ground. Look for their foraging pattern, which is often a repeated circular path around a cluster of houses or trees and often includes the entrance to their roost.

Big brown bat: A large bat with a wingspan of thirteen inches (325–350 mm.), this is the most familiar bat of the summer night. It begins foraging at dusk and flies in a steady, somewhat straight path about twenty to thirty feet above the ground. A big brown bat's flight pattern is often broken as it zips off course to capture insects. In a pattern similar to that of other kinds of bats, big brown bats fly over and over the same path each night. If you become familiar with some of these feeding paths, you will probably see the same bat flying there each night. These bats frequently are seen flying around the lights that line city streets.

Evening bats: The wingspan of these small bats is about ten inches (260–280 mm.). They begin foraging early in the evening and are plentiful around southern communities. Their slow flight and steady course make them easy to recognize after you have had some experience observing bats in flight. Not much is known about the feeding habits or the seasonal movements of these bats.

Mexican freetail bats: The span of their narrow wings is about eleven inches (290–325 mm.). When they leave their caves in Texas and New Mexico about fifteen minutes after sunset, they form a huge black cloud in the sky, and a roar like that of rushing water accompanies their departure from the roost. The flight is spectacular. Soon after leaving the cave, the bats go off in separate directions. These colonies are so large that some bats are just leaving as the first to exit begin to reenter the cave. They feed on small moths.

Pallid bat: Its wingspan is about fifteen inches (360–390 mm.), and it flies low, about three or four feet above the ground as it forages. Unlike other bats, these large-eyed bats hunt the ground for beetles and other insects.

Hoary bat: This is a large bat with a wingspan of about sixteen inches (380–410 mm.). Look for their straight and fast flight as they emerge late in the evening. Little is known about the eating habits of these attractive bats.

Red bat: The long, pointed wings that span about eleven inches (290–332 mm.) and its long tail in silhouette against the darkening sky are clues that you may be seeing this lovely reddish orange bat. These fast fliers have been clocked at forty miles per hour. When foraging, they fly low over treetops but will frequently hunt only a few feet above the ground. Red bats look for flies, true bugs, beetles, cicadas, and crickets. Although not much is known about their diets, the few known food preferences lead scientists to believe the little red bat hunts for some of its food on the ground. Not much is known about their habits.

Silver-haired bat: This medium-sized bat has a wingspan of about ten inches (270–310 mm.). Its flight is leisurely, and it cruises close to the ground and not above twenty feet. These bats may appear singly but are frequently found foraging in pairs. Because they are so difficult to find during the day, these bats, like so many others, have not been studied extensively, and most of their habits remain a mystery.

Is It a Bat or a Bird? Although swallows are active during the day, you may see them in the twilight as they skim the surfaces of ponds and streams. At this time, they are often mistaken for bats. (See Chapter Note 3.)

Common nighthawks (*Chordeiles minor*) are adept at catching insects while in flight. These avian fliers lead reclusive lives during the day but appear in the night sky in search of insects. These birds forage over open country, but you may see their silhouettes against the night sky in cities and towns. Scientists have found that bats and birds feast on caddisflies (trichopterans) and other insects, whereas both avoid midges (chironomids).

Whippoorwills feed extensively on moths and other insects caught on the wing. You may see these nightjars flying over woodlands that are close to open fields. When caught in the beam of automobile headlights, the birds' eyes reflect ruby red. Chuck-will's-widow flies over fields and low to the ground in its hunt for beetles, moths, winged ants, and termites. Look for these competitors in the evening sky.

With the help of the silhouettes below, try to identify the nighthawk, whippoorwill, and swallow while in flight. Compare their flight patterns with those of bats. Which of these night fliers do you think is most agile?

Battling Bats. Occasionally bats get into squabbles with one another. Although these confrontations are seldom serious, bats have been known to die as a result of them. If you should find a pair of battling bats, observe the strategies each uses to outwit the other. How do they use their arms? Do they make any noise? (See Chapter Note 4.)

Hanging. Most scientists believe that hanging upside down lets bats use spaces not inhabited by other animals, such as cave ceilings, undersides of tree limbs, and rock crevices. It may be an adaptation that protects them from predators.

swallow   whippoorwill   nighthawk

EXPLORATIONS

Do Bats Really Want to Dive into Your Hair? Bats don't really want to tangle with you or your hair. How close do you predict a bat will come to you before veering off? To find out, you will need some courage and a friend to help you. When you see a bat coming in your direction, remain still. Your friend can observe the flying bat to determine how close it gets. Try it again. Why do you think the bat doesn't hit you? (See Chapter Note 5.)

Building a Bat House. Many bats are losing their natural roosts. Building a bat house is one way you can encourage these friendly creatures of the night to come into your backyard. Better than the highly touted purple martin or an electric bug zapper at annihilating the mosquito, gnat, and moth populations, the bats will repay you for your consideration.

The directions for the bat house on the next page are taken from *America's Neighborhood Bats* by Dr. Merlin D. Tuttle. *Do not* use chemically treated wood for any part of your bat house.

Further Study. Because the study of bats has intensified only recently, these fascinating mammals have not been studied extensively. If you would like to dig deeper into the lives of bats, many museums and universities have excellent collections that may be available to you. A partial list of those institutions includes the American Museum of Natural History, New York, New York; the University of Michigan Museum of Zoology, Ann Arbor, Michigan; University of Kansas Museum of Natural History, Lawrence, Kansas; the Museum of Comparative Zoology, Harvard University, Cambridge, Massachusetts; and the University of California Museum of Vertebrate Zoology, Berkeley, California.

Questions Still to Be Answered. There are still many puzzles about bats. For example, how do bats find their way back to hibernating caves year after year and how does each find its particular location in those caves upon returning? It is known that bats avoid moths in the Arctiidae family. These moths produce ultrasonic clicks that keep the bat away but the exact mechanism involved is a mystery. We know where several species of bats gather but the locations where most bats gather and hibernate remain unknown. It's a fact that some bat species fly at specific altitudes, but it is not known if the bats do this because the insects they seek are found only at those altitudes. Some solitary bats return to the same roost night after night and year after year. How they find their way over hundreds of miles is another locked door that has not yet yielded to knocking investigators.

There are many, many other things to be discovered about the lives of bats. If you become interested in these night hunters of the sky, perhaps you

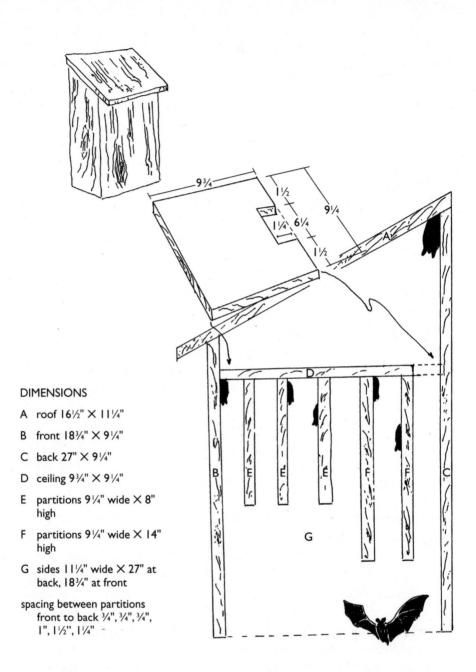

DIMENSIONS

A roof 16½" × 11¼"

B front 18¾" × 9¼"

C back 27" × 9¼"

D ceiling 9¾" × 9¼"

E partitions 9¼" wide × 8" high

F partitions 9¼" wide × 14" high

G sides 11¼" wide × 27" at back, 18¾" at front

spacing between partitions front to back ¾", ¾", ¾", 1", 1½", 1¼"

Use rough lumber and turn the rough sides of the roof, front, back, and sides inward. Cut ¹⁄₁₆ inch horizontal grooves at ½-inch intervals on smooth sides of partitions.

bat house

can add to the pool of bat knowledge. One way for you to increase your awareness about bats is to subscribe to the quarterly newsletter *Bat Research News*, which contains the latest news from the bat world. Write to the Department of Zoology, University of Kentucky, Lexington, KY 40506.

CHAPTER NOTES

1. Your Responsibility. Roosting or hibernating bats should not be disturbed. Intrusion by us during these crucial periods often means death for some of the bats. Frequently bats that have been severely disturbed will abandon the site and search for one that is more remote. This is especially unfortunate for the scientists that are studying the habits of the bats.

2. Teeth. The teeth of insect-eating bats are sharp and designed for tearing the tough outer covering (exoskeleton) worn by mosquitoes and other insects. Bats that dine exclusively on fruits don't have such prominent incisors. Scientists believe that early bats were all insect eaters as most of the bats found in North America are today. Through the thousands of years that bats have lived on earth, different food-gathering strategies have developed so that bats could fill additional niches by feeding on nectar, pollen, fruit, fish, and even small birds. These non-insect-eating bats live primarily in tropical regions.

3. Bats versus Swallows. Scientists have discovered that although both are insect eaters, swallows capture relatively few insects compared with the huge numbers caught by bats. The bat is designed for hunting insects at night, whereas the swallow fills that niche during the day. The swallow's poor eyesight in the dimming light and its technique of winnowing are no match for the bat's sonar system.

4. Bat Battles. The battle is usually fought while the bats are upside down. Arms are used for balance. Most of the sound produced is ultrasonic, so don't expect to hear squeals of protest.

5. Bats and You. Bats will avoid you because their tracking system tells them that you are too big to be a morsel of food. They know that an encounter with such a large object could be dangerous.

CHAPTER 9

Opossums

MYSTERIOUS MARSUPIALS

The opossum (*Didelphis marsupialis*) is one of our most misunderstood nocturnal mammals. Found throughout the United States and southern Canada, these shy animals usually avoid human observation even though they live in our backyards. Their reclusive habits, as well as their appearance—a long, pointed face with pink snout; beady eyes; pale, gray-white fur that's often tinged with a wash of yellow; and a hairless, ratlike tail covered with scales—have made the opossum a creature of myth and mystery.

The opossum's Latin name reflects its unique reproductive system—*didelphis* means "double uterus," and *marsupialis* means "pouch." (See Chapter Note 1.) The female adult opossum produces about twenty-two eggs at mating time, although she can produce as many as fifty-six. These eggs are so tiny that it would take about twenty-five of them to span the diameter of a quarter. Not all of the eggs produced are fertilized, and not all of the fertilized eggs will produce adult opossums.

As a marsupial, the opossum has an external pocket, or pouch, in which to carry its developing young. Opossum pups are born a mere twelve or thirteen days after conception, about the size of pencil erasers (less than one-half inch long) and the weight of two postage stamps ($1/175$ ounce). They are so immature that their hind limbs are merely tiny buds, they can neither see nor hear, and their bald skin is so transparent you can often see some of their internal organs. Using their one well-developed feature, front feet with five

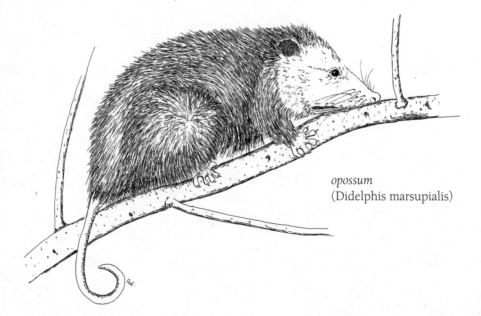

opossum
(Didelphis marsupialis)

This illustration of a newborn opossum is enlarged; in real life, the newborn is less than one-half inch long and looks like a hairless pink grub.

sharp claws, they crawl across the furry terrain of their mother's abdomen to the pouch. Although only a distance of two or three inches, this is a life-or-death journey for the half-inch-long newborns. Of all the pups born, only the first dozen to reach the pouch will survive.

This is so because within the opossum mother's pouch is a horseshoe of about twelve nipples, with an additional nipple near the center—there is no more room at the table. Even if a pup wanted to share some of the food with

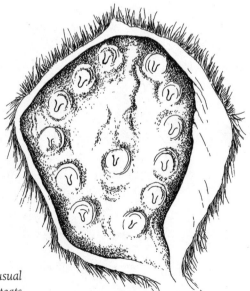

pouch opened to show usual position of teats

a latecomer it couldn't, because when a newborn begins to feed, the nipple swells so that the pup cannot remove it from its mouth. The beautifully designed newborn has strong cheek muscles so that it can suck in its first meal. (One myth surrounding the opossum held that opossum mothers used special abdominal muscles to pump milk into the pups. Scientists at Cornell University have proven this to be false.)

Opossum pups find warmth, nourishment, and safety in their mother's pouch for about three months. The mother can open and close the pouch to attend to her pups. When closed, the pouch is so well sealed that if the mother goes for a swim, the pups will stay dry and safe.

About sixty days after birth the young opossums open their eyes. By this time they are about the size of house mice (about six inches, including tail), and in another thirty days they will be weaned and no longer dependent on their mother for survival. At ninety days of age, the pups are about the size of chipmunks and ready to live on their own. Opossums living in the northern part of their range, from Washington, D.C., to southern Canada, generally have only one litter of pups each year; those living to the south have two and sometimes three litters annually.

The unusual characteristic of nurturing offspring in a pouch is shared by the kangaroo, the koala, and by some lesser-known animals such as wombats

Opossum pups ride on their mother's back, clinging to her hairs.

THE PLAYERS

duck-billed platypus, a monotreme
(Ornithorhynchus anatinus)

and bushtail possums (without the "o"), but the opossum is the only marsupial living in North America. All other North American mammals are placentals, which means their young develop within a saclike membrane called the placenta inside the mother's uterus, rather than in an exterior pouch. Cats, dogs, bears, lions, mice, and even humans are familiar placentals. Another, very rare, type of mammal called a monotreme has neither a placenta nor a pouch for the developing young, but lays eggs. The platypus, which lives in Asia and Tasmania, is a monotreme.

Opossums are among the most silent animals that live in the North American woodlands, but when frightened or threatened they growl and hiss. Even though opossums will snap their jaws and flash fifty needle-sharp teeth that can cause a painful wound, this may seem like meager protection when compared with the protective armor of the turtle, the spearlike quills of the porcupine, or the repulsive odor of the skunk. They also lack the speed to outrun such predators as foxes, wolves, and bobcats. Nevertheless, opossums are skilled at some very effective survival techniques.

Opossums are superb climbers. Each hind foot has an opposable toe, or thumb, which allows it to grasp objects. It can't press the thumb pad closed against its other fingers, however, so it's not able to pick up small things such as seeds. In addition to the marvelous thumb, opossums have a highly maneuverable tail, which allows them to move through the treetops with an astonishing agility equal to that of a high-wire performer. Once safely above the ground, an opossum can disappear into a tree cavity and remain there until the danger has passed.

If it is unable to escape a hungry predator, the opossum uses a curious trick to avoid being eaten—it "plays 'possum." This amazing animal is actually able to feign death.

It lies on its side, limp and seemingly lifeless, its eyes half closed and mouth open with tongue hanging out. It even smells dead, thanks to an odoriferous liquid excreted by a pair of anal glands. An opossum can remain "dead" for several hours if necessary, not moving a muscle even if poked, bitten, kicked, or even picked up and dropped with a thump. Scientists are unsure why opossums choose this prey-avoidance strategy or exactly what happens to them when they play dead. Recent study of opossum brain waves has shown that the animals do not hypnotize themselves into a stupor or experience a paralytic seizure, as was once thought.

Although the opossum was traditionally regarded as an animal of the American South, its range extends northward across the Canadian border, and in the early 1900s opossums were introduced along the Pacific coast. The opossum's expanded range is testimony to its adaptability. This successful little animal has benefited greatly from the sprawling human population. In the suburbs we provide them—often inadvertently—with an abundant

The right hind foot of an opossum. Note the "thumb" that permits the opossum to grasp objects.

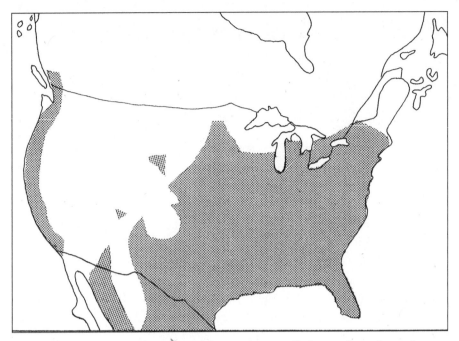

Opossums living in the northern part of their range generally have only one litter of pups each year; those living to the south have two or three.

supply of food that doesn't require them to hunt or depend on weather or time of year. Opossums that live in rural areas also find plenty of food and have been called "opportunistic omnivores" because they eat almost anything—grains, grasses, persimmons, wild grapes, apples, pokeberries, dewberries, seeds, sand, stones, earthworms, eggshells, birds, mollusks, insects, leaves, corn, amphibians, rabbits, and millipedes.

Although opossums live quite well in tree hollows and other natural places, they also find shelter in the basements, garages, barns, sheds, and porches that we have graciously provided. Good shelter is especially important for opossums, since they spend so much energy and time reproducing. Most opossums don't live more than one or two breeding seasons, and those that do live longer are often plagued by diseases such as cataracts.

Scientists are studying opossums to learn more about the health problems of both very young and very old humans. Because opossum newborns share similarities with human embryos, researchers are beginning to better understand the difficulties experienced by premature babies. In the future we may owe those silent nocturnal creatures that visit our trash cans a great deal from what we learn.

THE WORLD OF OPOSSUMS

What to Bring	Science Skills
basic kit	*observing*
camera	*recording*
rubber gloves	*inferring*
tenacity	

NOTE: Do not examine roadkill at night.

OBSERVATIONS

Where and When to Look. You can sometimes find opossums feasting on the carrion of roadkilled animals, a food source they seem to prefer. Unfortunately, this habit frequently results in their becoming roadkills themselves. Opossums are nocturnal except in the winter, when you can expect to find them foraging in the daylight during warm spells.

Observe an Opossum. Many biology teachers are directing their students toward the study of roadkill rather than using specimens ordered from biological supply houses. When examining a roadkilled opossum, use caution, wear reflective clothing, and be on the lookout for cars and trucks. If possible, use a shovel or stick to roll the carcass to the side of the road. Avoid touching the dead animal—you don't have to touch it to make accurate observations. What color is it? How big is it? Is it about as big as a medium-sized house cat or is it smaller than that? (See Chapter Note 2.) Describe the tail. What is the shape of the head? Is it boxlike, conical, round, or some other shape? If the opossum has an eye stripe, what color is it? What color are the ears? Are they covered with hair?

Describe the legs and feet. How many toes are there on each foot? Do all of the toes have claws? Describe the fur. Are all the hairs the same length and texture? (See Chapter Note 3.)

Pretend you are a reporter for a local newspaper. Your assignment is to write a piece about an unknown creature that was discovered on one of the roads in your neighborhood. Give your report to a friend. Based on your description, can your friend draw the animal or at least find a picture of it in a field guide? A few well-angled photographs will add to your report and are excellent additions to your field notebook.

Footprints. Opossums often frequent streams and other sources of fresh water. You frequently can find a set of opossum footprints in the mud or sand

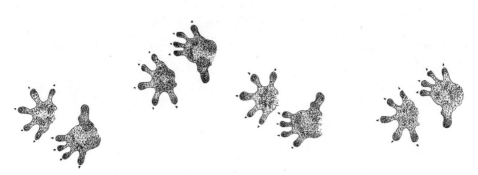

Look for opossum tracks in the mud or sand along the banks of streams.

that lines the banks of these watercourses. Some say that the prints resemble monkey prints, but that is not much help if you have never seen those. Look for prints that are similar to those in the illustration above. You may even see the print made from the tail as the opossum ambled along. Are the prints fresh? How do you know? Are there other footprints in the mud or sand. What animals do you think made them? What story can you tell from the footprints?

Home Range and Nests. Opossums are not territorial. This means that they do not defend a particular place as their own and therefore don't engage in the kind of territorial displays that other animals use to protect their turf. Most opossums wander alone from place to place each night as they forage.

Opossums build their nests in any place that suites their nomadic style, but the sites listed below are among their favorites.

Place	Materials	Habitat
Fallen logs	Leaves, grasses, cotton	Open woods, swamps, bogs, marshes, meadows, wet lowlands or wastelands, rocky cliffs, ledges, rock slides
Abandoned woodpecker holes or natural cavities in trees	Same as above	Woods, thickets, hedgerows
Abandoned skunk or woodchuck dens	Same as above	Woodlands, thickets, meadows

Opossums use their prehensile tails to carry nesting material.

Opossums use their prehensile (grasping) tails when gathering nest materials. If you have an opportunity to observe this, keep a record of what the opossum does. How does it use its mouth, front feet, hind feet, and tail? How long does it take the opossum to build the nest? (See Chapter Note 4.)

Is the Opossum Dead? "Playing 'possum" is a well-known behavior of the opossum. For many years this posture was thought to be the result of "suspended animation," but that notion has been discredited by scientific research. The opossum that is "playing dead" appears to be in a catatonic state, but its metabolic processes are as high as when the animal is fully alert.

When threatened, the opossum plays dead.

When the opossum believes the danger has passed, it begins to wake up, starting with the head. You can see this happen because the opossum will begin to wiggle its ears in an effort to pick up sounds. If it thinks the danger has passed, it will pick up its head and even look around. If danger persists, the opossum will play dead again.

If you should see an opossum in this state, it may look to you as though it has a spinal injury. Leave the opossum alone, because it is probably just waking up. If you are concerned about the animal, call a local wildlife specialist. (See Chapter Note 5.)

How Old Is That Opossum? Scientists often need to know the age of a particular animal so that they can figure out such things as the annual reproduction rate for a species, how long a species lives, and how long it takes to replace all the individuals in a population. For example, researchers have learned that in three years there is a complete turnover in the opossum population in a given area.

Some techniques used to determine the age of mammals are quite complicated and require the use of very sophisticated equipment, but by counting the teeth in an opossum, you can get some idea of how old it is. This is possible because teeth, along with certain bones and the lenses of the eyes, continue to grow even after general body growth has ceased.

Teeth. To determine the total number of teeth, push aside the lips of the roadkilled animal with a short, sturdy stick (or with your fingers while wearing rubber gloves). The total number of teeth includes incisors, canines, premolars, and molars. By ten months of age, opossums have a full set of fifty teeth, more than any other North American mammal. Use the following to determine the age of your opossum: thirty teeth = three months; forty teeth = four months; forty-four teeth = five months; forty-eight teeth = six to

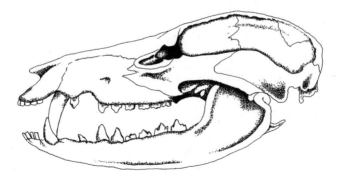

opossum skull—side view

seven months; fifty teeth = ten months. What is the approximate age of your opossum? (See Chapter Note 6.)

Dental Formula. A dental formula is a tool developed by scientists to identify an animal species. It includes the types of teeth, the way they are arranged, and the total number. In the formula, the first letter of each kind of tooth is used. A canine is represented by C, an incisor by I, a premolar by P, and a molar by M. The number of each kind of tooth on the upper jaw in one half of the mouth is represented from front to back by the appropriate letter followed by a number. For example, three incisors are identified as I 3, one canine as C 1, four premolars as P 4, and two molars as M 2. The number of each tooth on the lower jar is written below the number of the corresponding tooth found on the upper jaw. For example, the dental formula for a raccoon (*Procyon lotor*) is as follows:

$$I \frac{3}{3}, C \frac{1}{1}, P \frac{4}{4}, M \frac{2}{2}, = \begin{matrix} 10 \times 2 = 20 \text{ teeth on upper jaw} \\ 10 \times 2 = 20 \text{ teeth on lower jaw} \end{matrix}$$

The total number of teeth for *Procyon lotor* is 40.

Based on your observation, what is the dental formula for the opossum you have found? (See Chapter Note 6.) Write a dental formula for your teeth.

Pouch Fur. If you have the opportunity to observe an opossum pelt, look at the pouch. A shallow pouch lined with white fur is an indication of a young opossum that has not yet given birth to young. The mammary glands in these young opossums are white and very small. In an older opossum the pouch fur is rust colored, and generally some of it has been rubbed off by the movements of squirming young pups.

Roadkill and Age. Is there a relationship between the season of the year and the age of the opossums that you find? Have you found mature females or mostly males? You can identify the females by their abdominal pouches. (See Chapter Note 7.)

Top Speed. The word *marsupial* brings to mind visions of leaping Australian kangaroos that cover great distances with each bound. The little marsupial of North America could not compete in a race with such an animal unless it were given a handicap. How fast does the opossum travel? (See Chapter Note 8.)

When Opossums Breed. Based on the following chart, when would you predict opossums will mate in your area? How long will the mothers carry the young in their pouches? You can check your predictions by calling the extension service of the state university, a local zoo, a veterinarian, or the naturalists at your local nature center.

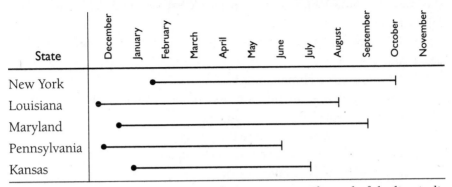

BREEDING SEASON FOR OPOSSUMS

State	December	January	February	March	April	May	June	July	August	September	October	November
New York				●————————————————————————						———		
Louisiana		●————————————————————————————										
Maryland			●——————————————————————————————————									
Pennsylvania			●————————————————————————									
Kansas				●————————————————————————								

Key: The ● indicates the earliest time for conception. The end of the line indicates the end of the "free ride" for the pups. You can find out more about this by consulting Walker's *Mammals of the World.*

Go to a Zoo. Many zoos are equipped with special windows and lighting that fool opossums and other nocturnal animals into thinking that day is night. If you have an opportunity to visit such a place, try to observe the animal grooming itself. Is there a pattern to the process? Observe a cat grooming. Does the opossum follow a similar pattern? Does it lick the forefeet and rub them all over its face as a cat does? How does it clean the rest of its body? (See Chapter Note 9.)

EXPLORATIONS

As scientists continue to observe the life and times of the opossum, many questions arise. Frequently amateur wildlife observers provide professional scientists with valuable information. By carefully recording your observations, you could help, too. Contact a nature center or a branch of a state university to find out the specifics for such a project. Following are some questions about the opossum that are being explored:

• Do newly weaned and juvenile opossums forage for the same or different foods than the adult opossums?

• What is the role played by opossums in suburban and urban wildlife populations?

• We know that death by cars and trucks is one cause of mortality. What are the other causes of death? Predators? Disease? Others?

• What effect do diet, climate, and the number of opossums in an area have on the number of litters per season and the number of newborns weaned in each litter?

Opossum Myths. Following are some myths about this elusive creature. (See Chapter Note 10 for corrections; see Chapman and Feldhamer in the Bibliography.)

1. The opossum is a living fossil, a holdover in North America from the age of dinosaurs.

2. The opossum is stupid.

3. Young opossums are not born like other mammals but are formed at the ends of the nipples like buds of a plant.

4. The mother pumps milk into the young.

5. The pup's lips and tongue fuse to the nipple.

6. A female rears three litters a year.

CHAPTER NOTES

1. Reproduction. The female opossum has two uteri, which accommodate the forked penis of the male. This anatomical structure differs from that of other mammal groups and was the seed of the myth that copulation took place through the female's nostrils. A related misconception held that newborn opossums were catapulted into the world in a great sneeze. Neither of these notions is true.

2. Size. The weight of adult opossums ranges from four to fifteen pounds, and body length may be twenty-four to thirty-four inches, including a ten- to thirteen-inch tail. Opossums are about the size of medium-sized house cats.

3. Descriptions. The opossum's head is cone shaped or conical and tapers to a pointed pink snout. Its fur may be various shades of gray and white and may have a wash of yellow. Some opossums have a grayish black eye stripe, and they may have a V-shaped wedge called a *widow's peak* that begins over the crown and runs toward the snout. Its black, leathery ears are hairless except at the edges. The eyes and ears of the opossum are about equal in prominence, which indicates that it probably relies equally on sight and hearing. In contrast, the bat has exceptionally large ears, which tell us that the bat finds its way in the dark of night through the sense of hearing.

The lower legs of the opossum are black, but its feet and toes are pinkish white. The forefeet have five clawed toes, whereas the hind feet have only four toes with claws. The first toe of each hind foot is large and opposable, which means it can be used like our thumbs. There is no claw or nail on this toe. The opossum's prehensile, or grasping, tail has been the source of many myths. It is long, scaly with few hairs, and creamy white except for a black patch at the base. Its ratlike appearance led early naturalists to believe that the opossum was a member of the rat family.

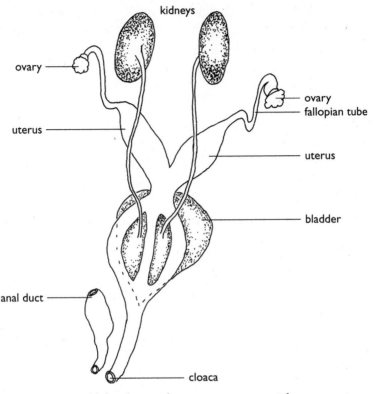

kidneys

ovary

ovary
fallopian tube

uterus

uterus

bladder

anal duct

cloaca

the female reproductive tract in marsupials

If you touch an opossum's fur, you will feel its coarseness. The top layer consists of long, white guard hairs; the undercoat is soft, white fur tipped with black. You may also notice that the guard hairs grow more thickly around the neck than on the rest of the body. An examination of a friendly neighborhood dog can give you a close-up view of the coarse guard hairs and the soft under-fur. A collie, Shetland sheepdog, or other long-haired dog is a good subject.

Although grayish white is the most common opossum color, they are sometimes black. This color is quite common in the southeastern part of the United States. In black opossums as much as one-half of the guard hairs are black, whereas in gray opossums the guard hairs are generally white.

4. Nests and Home Range. Opossums are not fussy about where they live as long as a source of fresh water is nearby. They build their nests in tree-trunk cavities, rocky crevices, hollow logs, abandoned skunk or woodchuck burrows, or brush heaps. When collecting nest material, the opossum gathers leaf litter with its mouth and passes it to its hind feet and then its tail. It then carries the nest material in a crook in its tail to the chosen site.

Opossums are nomads—they don't stay in any one area for a long time. They don't follow trails but wander in erratic pathways as they forage. This behavior has made it difficult for field biologists to keep track of individual opossums, but by using radio-tagged collars, a more accurate picture of opossum behavior can be assembled.

5. "Playing 'Possum." Some beetles, grasshoppers, spiders, birds, and foxes also "play 'possum," although most do not carry off the ruse as well as its namesake. Certain snakes, especially the West Indian wood snakes, feign death, and hog-nosed snakes that live in sandy regions of North America put on fairly good performances—until they are picked up. Then when dropped to the ground, they land on their bellies but quickly squiggle onto their backs, resuming their corpselike appearance. The opossum doesn't make such a foolish mistake.

6. More Fun with Teeth. The dental formula for an opossum (*Didelphis marsupialis*) is as follows:

$$\text{I } \frac{5}{4}, \text{ C } \frac{1}{1}, \text{ P } \frac{3}{3}, \text{ M } \frac{4}{4} = 50$$

7. Roadkill Statistics. In the summer to early fall you can expect to find seven young opossums killed for every adult female. By winter this ratio has decreased to six young per adult female. In the wild most opossums apparently live no more than two years. It is estimated that it takes three and one-half years for the population of a given area to be replaced by new individuals.

8. Other Mammals and Speed. The opossum has a top speed of about four miles per hour. Compare this with the gray squirrel, which races along the ground at about seventeen miles per hour but is somewhat slower when running through the treetops, and the chipmunk, which tears along the woodland floor at about ten miles per hour. You could time these animals and see if, on average, your results are similar.

9. Grooming. An opossum uses its hind foot in much the same way as we use a washcloth. It grooms its ears, the back of its head, and its upper body with a foot that is licked clean throughout the process. The opossum uses its fine set of claws for combing its hair. Its forefeet are used to clean its face. Licking gets the abdomen and genital area clean, and if young are in the pouch, the mother keeps that area very clean by licking it thoroughly. If you cannot find an opossum to watch, the neighborhood feline will put on a copycat performance.

10. Corrections

1. All marsupials originally inhabiting North America became extinct by the mid-Tertiary period. The first record for the opossum is late Pleistocene period.

2. Opossums are inhibited animals, especially in daylight or under artificial light, but are by no means stupid. Results from some learning and discrimination tests rank opossums above dogs and more or less on a par with pigs in intelligence

3. Young are born like other mammals, although in a relatively underdeveloped condition.

4. The young suckle without aid from the mother.

5. The pouch young become firmly attached to the nipples, but no fusion occurs. The false observation is based on the bloody, sometimes torn mouth that results when young are not carefully removed. To avoid damage to the young, researchers have suggested gently twisting to "unscrew" them from the nipple.

6. There is no evidence that the opossum successfully rears more than two litters a year. Females may give birth to three or more litters during a season if earlier litters are lost.

CHAPTER 10

Hoppers

FRIENDS OR FOES?

Grasshoppers are found wherever there are grasses—in the desert, at the seashore, and in the mountains. They are most abundant in warm and sunny areas such as fields, meadows, and prairies. Crickets and katydids frequent these habitats as well, but these hoppers achieve their greatest diversity in woodlands. Throughout the ages these insects have been a part of man's surroundings and, sometimes, their diets. Although they are no longer desirable in Western cuisine, this may change. At a "bug banquet" hosted by the New York Entomological Society, guests dined on cricket and vegetable tempura. Grasshopper soup was featured at the annual meeting of another science society. The guests at these special events reported delight and surprise at the unusual fare.

Our relationship with grasshoppers has not always been so satisfying. A brief review of history tells us that grasshoppers can be a scourge. Great swarms of them periodically devour every green thing in farmlands of Asia and Africa and on the American plains. They have fed from these and other banquet tables since long before the biblical plagues of locusts (grasshoppers) in Egypt.

Evidence that this has been going on for thousands of years was discovered in glacial ice high in the Rocky Mountains in the northern section of Yellowstone National Park. Every year the summer sun thaws the leading edge of "Grasshopper Glacier," releasing thousands of grasshoppers from their icy tomb. With the help of carbon dating, scientists have learned that the grasshoppers were trapped when flying over the ice up the windward side of the mountain. The temperature quickly drops below the freezing point at high altitudes; grasshoppers cannot fly in those conditions, so they crashed onto the glacier. Their bodies were quickly covered with snow, and ultimately they formed the dark bands seen today in that glacial ice. They remained locked in the ice for many centuries as the glacier slowly moved down into the warmer valley.

Plagues of grasshoppers, primarily from the genera *Schistocerca* and *Locusta*, occur periodically in various parts of the world, and for most of recorded history the appearance of these vast swarms was cloaked in mystery. Scientific detective work has produced an explanation of this phenomenon. Grasshoppers (*Melanoplus* sp.) can live quietly in small numbers for years in arid areas. They are not very social and prefer to forage away from others of their kind. As adults, their drab bodies support small wings and underdeveloped leg muscles. They never travel far from the place where they hatched. Because their habitat is normally dry, the amount of water available is only enough to ensure the successful hatching of a few eggs, keeping the population small. There is a balance here because the minimal rainfall generally supports a limited crop of grasses and the other kinds of vegetation the locusts use for food.

Every so often, perhaps once in fifteen or twenty years, rainfall is unusually high. This changes the balance within the ecosystem and a curious thing happens to the locusts. Huge numbers of eggs hatch. Although of the same species, this generation differs from previous ones in amazing ways. The new locusts are darker in color and, instead of being shy and solitary, seek each other out and form enormous groups. As adults, the locusts have longer wings and very well developed leg muscles. They also are very social, feeding together on the now abundant vegetation until they strip everything bare and, still hungry, become airborne.

These locusts are not powerful fliers, but strong prevailing winds will move millions of them across the land. At this point they are a real danger to crops growing downwind of their once arid birthplace, and are virtually unstoppable.

Swarms of locusts have been found at elevations as high as 20,000 feet, looking like dark clouds on the horizon. The swarms contain hundreds of millions of insects and weigh thousands of tons. It's been said that each day a ton of locusts can eat as much as 250 people or 10 elephants. Just imagine the results of having 10,000 elephants drop into a farming community for a meal!

When the locusts are carried by winds over favorable feeding grounds, they fall out of the sky like a hungry black snowstorm. They eat absolutely every green thing: crops, grasses, leaves, shrubs. So huge are these swarms that they have been known to block highways and railway lines—this is especially dangerous because grasshopper bodies are very oily. Some swarming grasshoppers have been caught in offshore winds and carried out to sea. As they fall into the sea many of them become food for fish, and the bodies of others are heaped onto waterfront beaches.

These locusts are called short-horned grasshoppers because their antennae are shorter than their bodies. Katydids and cone-headed and meadow grasshoppers have antennae that are longer than their bodies and are therefore called long-horned grasshoppers. Long-horned grasshoppers are more closely related to crickets than they are to short-horned grasshoppers. You will have an opportunity to learn more about these different insects in the activities that follow.

Like all insects, grasshoppers, crickets, and katydids have three body

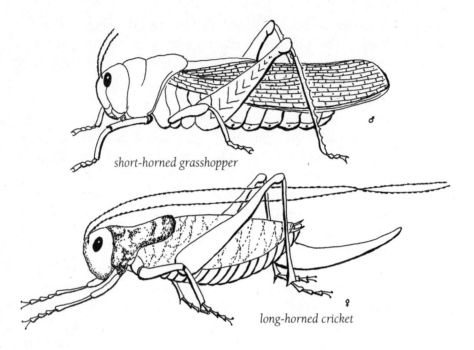

short-horned grasshopper

long-horned cricket

parts (head, chest, and abdomen) and three pair of legs. These traits distinguish them from the eight-legged spiders (arachnids) and the many-legged centipedes (chilopods). Grasshoppers, crickets, and katydids belong to the large order called Orthoptera (from the Greek words *ortho,* meaning "straight," and *ptera,* meaning "wing"), which contains about 20,000 different species found throughout the world. One noteworthy characteristic of orthopterans is the way they develop from eggs into adults in a three-stage development process called incomplete, or simple, metamorphosis. The changes that occur during growth and development are less dramatic than those of insects such as moths and butterflies that experience complete metamorphosis. In each of the four stages of that process—egg, larva (caterpillar), pupa, and adult—the insect assumes a completely different appearance. In incomplete metamorphosis the insect changes in size but not much in overall appearance.

After hatching from eggs, young grasshoppers, crickets, and katydids—called *nymphs*—look very much like adults but are smaller and different colors. They also lack wings and fully developed sex organs. As the nymphs develop, they molt several times—that is, they shed their rigid external coats, made of a hard substance called chitin, because the coats can't stretch to

life cycle of a cricket

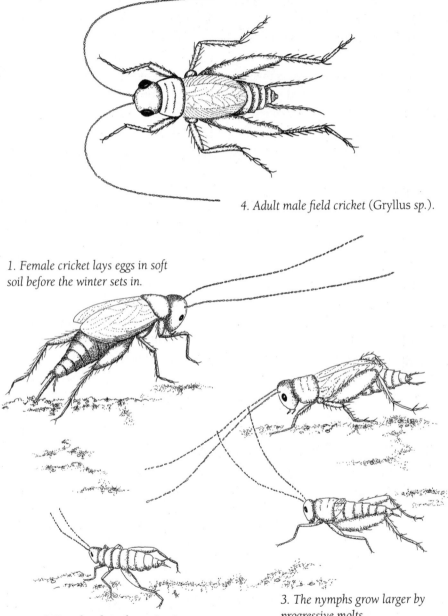

4. *Adult male field cricket* (Gryllus *sp.*).

1. Female cricket lays eggs in soft soil before the winter sets in.

3. The nymphs grow larger by progressive molts.

2. Eggs hatch in the spring into young crickets, called nymphs.

accommodate the growing insect bodies. Molting is triggered by hormones, and eventually the insect grows a new hard "skin," which protects the soft body parts that lie underneath. The joints are flexible, but the places where muscles are attached are rigid. Immediately after shedding its old armor, the insect is very vulnerable—a soft morsel preferred by many predators. It is also in danger of drying out before the new covering is formed. To prevent this fatal possibility, insects usually molt in the early morning, when the humidity is normally high. A thin film of wax secreted through minute pores covers the body armor and protects it from abrasion much the way we protect the paint on our cars by applying wax.

In the sixty or so days that it takes grasshoppers to reach maturity, they molt about five times. Crickets require sixty to ninety days to mature, shedding their "skin" five to twelve times in the process.

Orthopterans are probably best known for their jumping ability and their evening music that fills the countryside, especially during late summer when the birds have ceased calling and the great choruses of frogs are silent. Although you can hear the bell-like chirps of the ground cricket and the synchronous trills and tinkles of the "Orthopteran Symphony Orchestra" tuning up throughout the day, it is during the evening hours that their music reaches its great crescendo. These tiny musicians have provided background music for our outdoor parties and have lulled many of us to sleep with their chirps, lisps, buzzes, and whistles. As summer yields to autumn and the nights grow cooler, each species is silenced in its own time. In late autumn only a few lone ground crickets remain to play their bell-like chirps until the hard frost ends another season, and winter silence reclaims the land.

THE WORLD OF HOPPERS

What to Bring	Science Skills
basic kit	*observing*
insect net	*recording*
wide-mouthed gallon jar with lid	*comparing*
tape recorder	*measuring*
determination	

OBSERVATIONS

A Little Night Music. Although orthopterans and their "music" are associated with autumn evenings, you can find grasshoppers, crickets, and katydids throughout the summer. As you become more aware of their sounds, you will also notice that some of them begin to play as early as June, whereas others don't begin tuning up until later in the season. The sounds listed in the chart below are based on those reported by different observers. The phonetics may help you sort the sounds into major groups. To identify a specific grasshopper by its sound, you will need to relate the "tune" with the habitat and season of the year.

Insect	Season*	Sound
Northern true katydid (*Pterophylla camellifolia*)	Mid-August to early November	"Katydid . . . katydid . . . did"
Field cricket (*Gryllus* sp.)	Early May to early November	Clear, musical chirp or trill
Carolina ground cricket (*Eunemobius carolinus*)	Early August to mid-November	Stuttering, uneven trill
Tinkling ground cricket (*Allonemobius tinnulus*)	Early August to October	Soft, high-pitched tinkling sound, pulsating trills
Tree crickets (in general) (*Oecanthus* sp.)	End of July to end of October	Loud chorusing trills, like spring peepers
Snowy tree cricket (*Oecanthus fultoni*)	Same as other tree crickets	Chirps (only tree cricket that does this)
Meadow grasshopper (*Orchelimum* sp.)	End of July to end of October	Buzzes followed by six to nine clicks
Band-winged grasshopper (*Dissosteira carolina*)	Mid-July to end of October	Buzzes, clicks, snaps, and crackles on takeoff and in flight
Cone-headed grasshopper (*Neoconocephalus* sp.)	August to end of September	High-pitched buzz, continues for minutes at a time

* The end of the season for many grasshopper species coincides with the date of the first hard frost.

The Concert. Temperature is the conductor of this great insect orchestra, so it is no surprise that the musicians begin tuning up for their nocturnal concerts during the warmth of late afternoon and early evening. With the passing hours, more and more join in. When does the orchestra seem to reach a crescendo? At what time does the orchestra begin to lose some of its players? When is the concert over for the night? (See Chapter Note 1.) What is the relationship between temperature and the playing of the symphony?

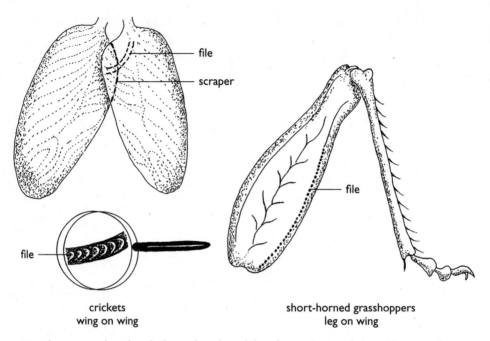

| crickets | short-horned grasshoppers |
| wing on wing | leg on wing |

Grasshoppers and crickets lack vocal cords and therefore make sounds by rubbing together parts of their bodies.

The Musical Instruments. Hoppers "sing" by rubbing two body parts together in a process called *stridulation*. Crickets make sounds by rubbing the bases of their wings together; short-horned grasshoppers rub their hind legs against the ridges on their front wings. No hoppers make sounds by rubbing their legs together, as was once thought. You can examine the "instrument" of a dead cricket by removing its wings and looking for the file near the base of one of the wings and the scraper close to the base of the other. Can you make a sound by rubbing these two structures together? Crickets can adjust the volume of their sounds by the shape of the trumpetlike funnel created by the forewings.

How Many Different Musicians? Although you can hear the insect "musicians" playing during the day, the full orchestra generally doesn't gather until late evening. Each species produces a unique sound. Listen for whistles, chirps, buzzes, lisps, trills, and tinkling sounds. Make a list of the different sounds you hear. Each time you listen, try to pick out some new sounds to add to your list.

Where Do the Different "Musicians" Play? Just as violins, clarinets, and other instruments have assigned positions in our orchestras, each species of hopper plays only from specific areas of vegetation. Describe the sounds you hear coming from ground level, from tall weeds, from ten to fifteen feet above the ground in small trees and shrubs, and from taller trees. The chart below lists the insects that play in each layer.

Insects	Ground	Tall Grasses, Weeds	Shrubs	Tall Trees	Day or Night
Northern true katydid 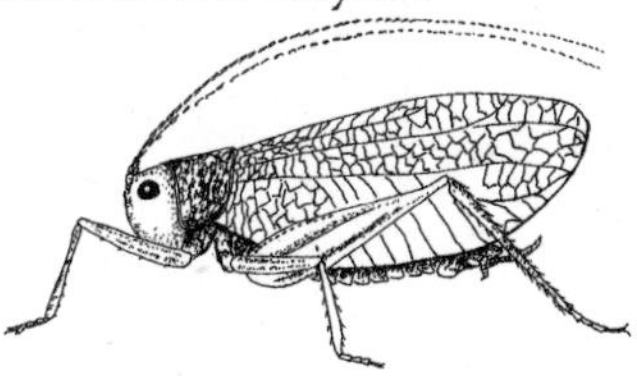				X	N
Field cricket 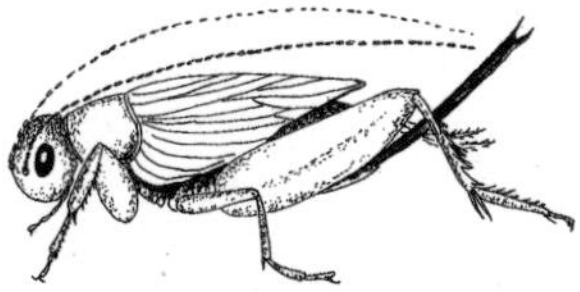	X				D,N
Tinkling ground cricket 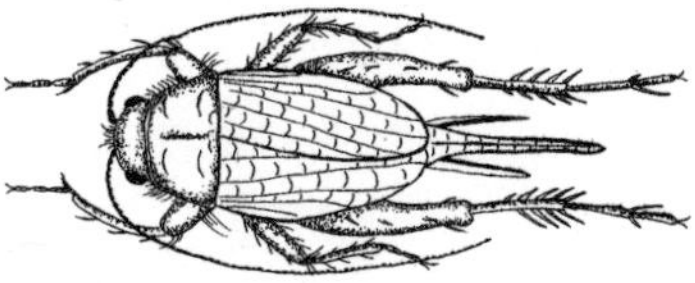	X				N
Snowy tree cricket 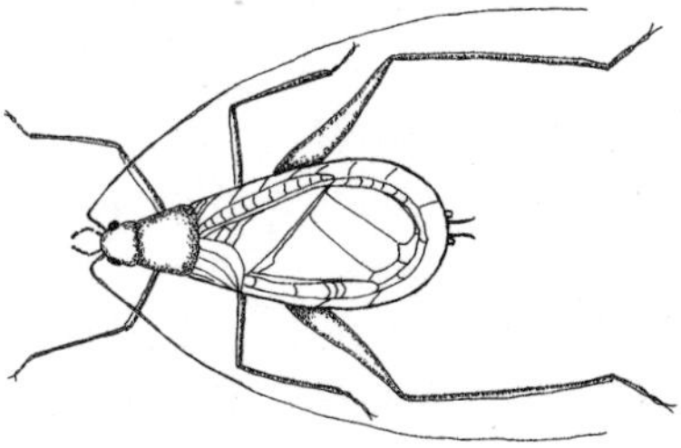			X	X	D,N
Tree crickets 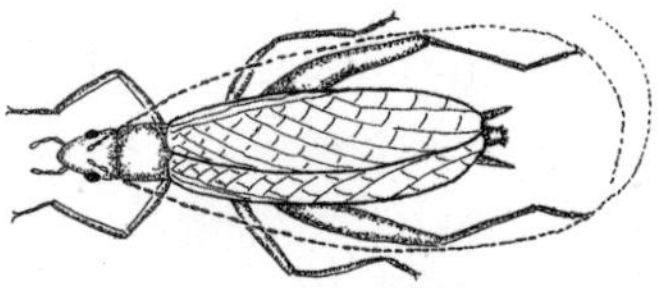		X	X	X	D,N

Insects	Ground	Tall Grasses, Weeds	Shrubs	Tall Trees	Day or Night
Common meadow grasshopper		X			D,N
Cone-headed grasshopper		X			N
Band-winged locusts	X dry, gravelly, along the roadside				D

Grasshoppers don't make much music, and we hear them during daylight. Crickets and katydids are more musical, and they call at night more than by day.

Don't be discouraged if you cannot always successfully locate individual insects by their sounds; many are superb ventriloquists and may not be where they seem to be. These noisy insects have developed strategies to protect themselves from predators: Pattern and color provide excellent protection for some, and many that live in foliage resemble leaves. Others escape from hungry predators by remaining perfectly quiet when danger is near, and still others rely on rapid flight to make quick getaways.

Who's Who? Trying to figure out who's who in the world of grasshoppers, crickets, and katydids can be very confusing. To simplify your task, begin by dividing the hoppers you capture into two groups. The chart below will help you to organize your collection. (See Chapter Note 2.)

ORTHOPTERANS

Short-horned Grasshoppers (Locusts) Caelifera Family	Katydids (Long-horned Grasshoppers) and Crickets Ensifera Family
Spur-throated grasshopper (e.g., lubber grasshopper) Band-winged grasshopper (e.g., Carolina locust) Slant-faced grasshoppers	Meadow katydids Cone-headed katydids Northern true katydid Crickets: field, ground, tree

One way to simplify terminology is to call all tettigoniids katydids (e.g., cone-headed katydids, meadow katydids, true katydids, and bush katydids). (Tettigoniidae is the family name for long-horned grasshoppers and katydids.)

EXPLORATIONS

How to Collect. Because grasshoppers are most abundant in late summer and autumn, plan to observe them at this time. A good way to begin systematic observation is to capture a grasshopper. Take a walk in a grassy field or meadow and scores of insects will fly up from the grass as you move through it. Catch a grasshopper with an insect net or your hand. When you have a captive or two, put each directly into a plastic sandwich bag so that you can observe and compare them.

How many short-horned and long-horned grasshoppers did you capture?

Closer Look. Grasshoppers are large (especially if you trap them late in the season), usually easy to capture, and survive well in a container for a short period of time. Take a close look at your grasshopper, and with the help of the illustration discover some of the physical features that make this insect work so well in its environment.

Head

Mouthparts: With the help of a hand lens, look for the jaws (mandibles and maxillae). Watch as the hopper eats a blade of grass. The northern true katydid (*Pterophylla camellifolia*) holds its food in its front claws and nibbles rather than tearing its food the way that short-horned grasshoppers do.

Eyes: Grasshoppers have two sets of eyes. This is handy because the grasshopper cannot adjust its eyes for far and near vision in the way that we can. The two large compound eyes are for distance vision and are composed

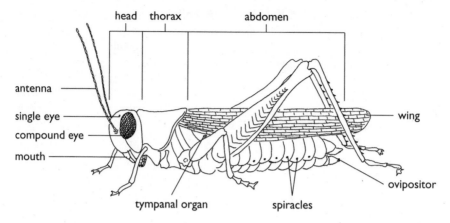

external structure of a grasshopper

of thousands of little lenses and other eye parts. Compare the eyes in the illustration with those of the grasshopper you have caught.

Antennae: Are the antennae longer or shorter than the grasshopper's body? If they are longer, how much longer are they? With the help of a hand lens, you can see the many joints that make the antennae so flexible. What does the insect do with the antennae? Put some food in the path of the grasshopper so that the antennae can reach it. What happens? (See Chapter Note 3.)

Thorax. A grasshopper has six legs. The first pair are short. Watch as the grasshopper walks up the side of a glass. With a hand lens observe the tiny feet. Look for hairy pads on each claw. The hairs secrete a sticky liquid that prevents the hopper from slipping when walking on smooth surfaces. The second pair of legs are somewhat longer than the first. The third pair are long and muscular and ideal for jumping. Look for double pairs of spines on the back of each hind foot. These aid in jumping by digging into the ground like the cleats on a sprinter's shoes.

Observe the grasshopper walking. A usual pattern when walking is for the grasshopper to take two steps forward, then stop; take another two steps forward, then stop; and so forth. If the hind legs are moving slowly, the other legs are moving at a similar pace. What happens to the front legs when the hind legs are moving more rapidly?

Abdomen. The abdomen is divided into segments. These segments hint at the grasshopper's relationship to annelids (worms). Do the rings go around the entire body? Lift the wings and find the hearing organ on the first segment of the abdomen.

Look for breathing pores along the side of the abdomen. How many are there? (See Chapter Note 4.)

Breathing. Look carefully and you will see the abdomen move rhythmically up and down. If one up-and-down cycle equals one breath, how many breaths does a grasshopper take each minute? Is this the same number of breaths that you take each minute, or is it more or fewer?

Grooming. While you are observing your grasshoppers, you may be able to watch the grooming process. Does there appear to be a sequence to the process, or is it haphazard? How does the grasshopper clean its antennae, its wings, its legs, and its body? Compare grooming among the different grasshoppers you find. Field crickets are probably the least fastidious.

Chemical Self-Defense. If you have ever handled a grasshopper, you may have already discovered their very effective chemical weapon. If not, you can expect a surprise as you continue to handle them. The chemical released by the grasshopper will not harm you. (See Chapter Note 5.)

Observations at Home. If you want to continue your observations at home, transfer your grasshoppers to a larger container such as a wide-mouthed gallon jar. Put a small handful of grasses into the jar to supply the grasshoppers with food and a familiar habitat. Fill a small vial with water and use a piece of cotton as a stopper, making sure the end of the cotton is in contact with the water. Capillary action will draw the water into the cotton so that the grasshoppers can drink from it.

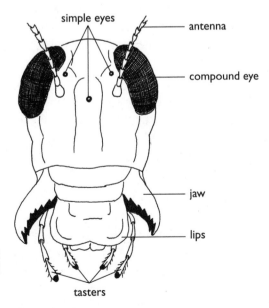

close-up of a grasshopper's head

Rasps per Minute. When you hear the familiar rasp "Katydid . . . she-did . . . she-did" of the northern true katydid, count the rasps for fifteen seconds and multiply that number by four to determine the rasp rate per minute. Do you notice a difference in calling frequency between warm and cool nights? It has been reported that a katydid rasps between 30 million and 50 million times in a season. The file and scraper are not worn away because they are made of chitin, a protein-based material that is highly resistant to erosion. The chitin is also very light, an asset for the flying arthropods.

Capture a Field Cricket. Field crickets are lively and run through leaf litter with amazing speed. They are not as shy as their cousins that live in the shrubbery or in the trees and are fairly easy to capture by hand even though they are quite slippery. Follow their chirp, but move slowly—if they sense you coming they will stop calling. You can expect to hear them chirping early in the spring, a good time to catch one. Later in the summer it is often difficult for the beginner to identify this cheery song because it is last among so many other hopper tunes.

A Cricket Home. A cricket cage is easy to prepare. Put some soil and grass into a medium-sized glass or plastic container. Add some water to a shallow pan or jar lid and put it into the cage. A small piece of rotting wood will provide a place for the cricket to hide and perhaps fashion a burrow. Field crickets eat small amounts of meat and vegetables.

Male versus Female. Female field crickets can be identified by their long, needlelike ovipositors, used to penetrate soil where they lay their eggs. The ovipositor is located between two sensor appendages that also protrude from the rear end. These structures pick up vibrations from the ground and warn of possible danger. You can identify male field crickets by the absence of the ovipositor or the presence of front wings specialized for singing.

Three Cricket Songs. Male black field crickets are territorial, so if you capture two or three males, house them in separate containers. Listen to the tune the males sing. Will they sing together (synchronously)? Put two males into the same container. What happens? Is there a difference in the tune they sing? What do the crickets do when they argue over territory? Put a female cricket in the cage with one chirping male cricket. Listen for the tune the male sings. Is this tune different than the other tunes? (See Chapter Note 6.)

Cricket Habitats. Male crickets are fiercely independent and rule over a small territory. You can find their burrows under clumps of grass and in cracks in logs or walls. It is not unusual for them to sing in a corner of the basement, garage, or even in the living-room fireplace. You might find them reigning under leaf litter or a piece of rotting fruit. From these places a male cricket may chirp almost continuously.

Can You Fool a Cricket? Female crickets are attracted to males of the same species. Record the sound of a male field cricket. (See Chapter Note 7.) Play the record or tape and release a female cricket in your room. What does the female cricket do? After you have made your observations, return her to the container.

Bring a male cricket in a container into the room where you have the female cricket. When the male cricket begins to chirp, release the female again. What does she do? Play the recording at high volume. Does the female seem to prefer the live cricket or the recording?

The Cricket Walk. The black field cricket cannot fly. It has very short wings under the wing covers, or forewings. Crickets are very agile (as you may have discovered when you tried to catch them). As you watch crickets, you may be surprised at how much time they spend walking or running from place to place.

You will notice that when a leg is in the air, the leg directly behind is on the ground. As you observe the insect walking, can you determine the function of its front pair of legs? Its hind legs? The middle pair of legs? (See Chapter Note 7.)

Right-handed Crickets? Although most crickets chirp by placing the right forewing over the left forewing, some crickets reverse the process. Are any of your crickets left-handed? Katydids generally are.

Snowy Tree Cricket. Snowy tree crickets are the only tree crickets that chirp. Their sound is soft and quite pretty. Listen for it in the early evening. At first there is only one, but soon there will be another, then another, until the whole area is filled with their sweet sound. As each male joins the chorus, it becomes in synchrony with the others; they sound like a great chorus with all the members singing in unison. Their songs begin late in August and continue each evening through October.

CHAPTER NOTES

I. The Schedule. The orchestra is playing full by midnight. From then on it loses members until only a few sounds linger in the predawn air. As you spend time listening, you will be able to recognize the tunes of those hoppers that remain. You may hear the chirp, chirp of the cricket silenced by the voice of predawn robins, but crickets will return in force by early afternoon if rain, cold, or extreme heat doesn't quell their enthusiasm.

2. Sorting the Hoppers

Short-horned Grasshoppers. The hoppers in this group belong to the family Acrididae. As their name implies, their antennae are shorter than the length of the body. Members of this group include band-winged locusts and slant-faced locusts. The female lays its eggs with its blunt, chisel-shaped ovipositor, which resembles an appendage protruding from the end of the abdomen between the hind legs.

Long-horned Grasshoppers. This group of hoppers includes such notables as the field crickets, ground crickets, cone-headed grasshoppers, bush katydids, meadow grasshoppers, true katydids, and tree crickets. (In general, crickets are never grasshoppers.)

3. Antennae. Antennae are equipped to detect odors; insects depend on antennae to identify food. Antennae are the insect equivalent of a very directional, mobile nose and are in constant motion. Generally an insect that has poor eyesight has large antennae.

4. Respiratory System. Insects breathe air through a system of tracheal tubes, which branch and rebranch into a complex system that conducts oxygen directly to all organs of the body. Blood is not important in the respiration of grasshoppers. If left underwater too long, the grasshopper will drown.

5. Chemical Warfare. Grasshoppers can produce a foul-smelling liquid commonly called "tobacco juice," which they spit at would-be predators. The juice seems to repel some attacks. A chemical analysis suggests that naturally occurring toxins from the plants that grasshoppers eat are incorporated into this juice. Research suggests that insecticides are also part of this excretion.

6. Types of Songs. Male field crickets play three different tunes—calling, courtship, and aggression. With practice and patience you can learn to identify these three different tunes. Female field crickets do not play music. This distinction between the sexes is true of other grasshoppers as well.

7. Source of Commercial Recordings. For information about custom-made tapes or CDs of insect sounds, contact the Cornell Laboratory of Ornithology, 159 Sapsucker Woods Road, Ithaca, NY 14850, phone (607) 254-2407.

8. Leg Movement. A cricket uses its front legs for grasping and pulling, and its back pair of legs for pushing. The middle pair serve as a fulcrum or pivot. A cricket's walk thus has a wavelike motion. Let a cricket walk through a few drops of food coloring. Make a diagram of the footprints made by your cricket.

CHAPTER 11

Raccoons

MISCHIEF MAKERS

It is the dead of winter and most of the wild world is still. In the hollow of an old tree a male raccoon (*Procyon lotor*) stirs, awakened by his internal timepiece. That hormonal clock tells him he must rise and seek a mate. In the quiet of the frosty night, he makes his way down the tree trunk and listens to the woods echo with the eerie courtship calls of the barred owl. The babbling brook of summer has been frozen into silence, and hunger stalks the snow-covered woodland. Some distance from his nest, a female raccoon denned in the cavity of an old oak tree also wakes up. The breeding season has begun.

In their drive to find a mate, male raccoons sometimes squabble over a particular female—and the winner doesn't necessarily "get the girl." When a female raccoon does finally accept a male as her mate, he enters her den and courts her for about two weeks. Shortly thereafter she drives him away, and he begins his search for another mate. Once the male is gone, the now-pregnant female goes back to sleep until spring.

Most raccoons mate between January and March, but those living in colder regions begin mating somewhat later than raccoons that live in the South. Most litters are born in April, but those kits that were conceived late in the breeding season won't arrive until midsummer. These latecomers born in the North frequently cannot store enough fat to sustain them throughout

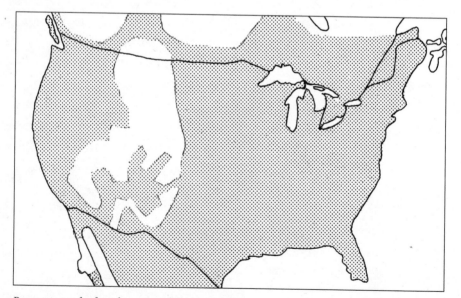

Raccoons can be found in most of the United States except portions of the Rocky Mountain states, central Nevada, and Utah.

Kits tag close to their mother's heels and copy her as she forages.

the long northern winter; as you might expect, their late-arriving southern cousins have a better survival rate.

About two weeks prior to the birth of the kits, the mother raccoon chews and scratches the soft rotting wood from the wall of her den and adds it to her own shed hair to fashion a nest. Raccoons that live in coastal areas where suitable trees are not available give birth in ground nests located in clumps of tall grasses, or in abandoned muskrat houses.

Sometime between sixty and seventy-three days after mating, the female raccoon gives birth to three to seven kits. A newborn kit can fit into the palm of your hand and weighs a mere two to three ounces (sixty to seventy-five grams). These tiny, hairless kits enter the world with eyes and ears sealed and must wait about eighteen days before they can see their mother. Baby raccoons remain in the tree den until they are about ten weeks old, when they can run and climb and accompany their mother on nightly sorties in search of berries, insects, and small aquatic animals. A mother and her kits may move from the old tree to a den on the ground as the young become more active.

A raccoon mother is an attentive caregiver. She meets all of the basic needs of the newborns, and as they grown older she teaches them how to forage and avoid predators, as well as other survival skills. Raccoon mothers will also adopt orphaned kits.

Raccoon kits usually stay with their mother throughout the summer and fall. When winter arrives, the mother and her brood generally sleep together in one den, although many raccoons prefer to overwinter alone. By denning together, the young raccoons have a better chance of survival because they keep each other warm. If you were to watch a group of raccoons sleep, you would notice frequent movement in this heap of fur as those on the outside of the pile wiggled their way into the center when they got cold, exposing others to the chilled air.

Although raccoons sleep during much of the winter, they don't hibernate. True hibernators, such as woodchucks, shrews, and bats, experience radical physiological changes; their metabolic rate may be reduced to $1/75$ of its normal level, their respiration often drops to less than one breath per minute, their body temperature may fall fifty degrees, and their heart rate slows. Raccoons maintain most of their normal body processes, but like skunks and bears, they alternate between sleep and wakefulness and are not active during periods of extreme cold. Throughout the winter, raccoons leave their nests in search of food, but if a raccoon pokes its head out of the tree hollow and sees the land under a blanket of snow, it is likely to go back to sleep. Raccoons become accustomed to the cold as the winter wears on. Early in the season they rarely venture out if the temperature is below thirty degrees F. Later, however, it is not unusual for raccoons to be out on nights when the mercury drops to a few degrees above zero. As the winter grows old, raccoons spend more time away from their dens looking for food.

The arrival of spring brings reorganization to the raccoon family as competition for space and food grows keen. The mother raccoon chases her yearlings away. If they have learned their lessons well, they are skillful hunters and know some tricks that will keep them safe from such enemies as bobcats (*Lynx rufus*), coyotes (*Canis latrans*), great horned owls (*Bubo virginianus*), fishers (*Martes pennanti*), and mountain lions (*Felis concolor*). With luck they should live six or more years.

Like bears, foxes, wolves, skunks, ferrets, badgers, cats, and dogs, raccoons are omnivores, which means they eat both plants and animals. The young raccoons will hunt for their favorite foods—insects and small vertebrate animals, as well as acorns and berries. All omnivores are equipped with special teeth called *canines* that are located next to the incisors and in front of the premolars. These large, cone-shaped teeth are well adapted for grabbing and tearing flesh. If you look in a mirror and smile at yourself, you can get a good look at a set of four very effective canines. How do yours compare with those of a dog or a cat? What are some probable explanations for the differ-

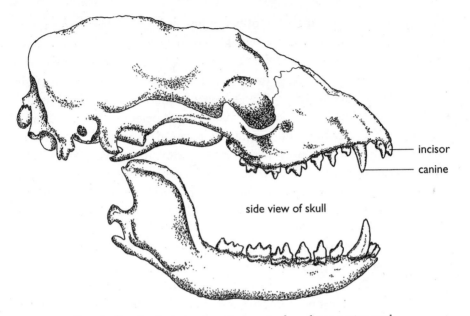

As with all animals that eat meat, raccoons have large canine teeth.

ences you notice? In mythology, folks like Count Dracula had especially well-developed canines.

Scientists have classified raccoons as belonging to the Canine order and the Procynoidae family. Their close relatives are the coati *(Nasua narica),* of the southwestern United States and Mexico. Unlike the nocturnal raccoon, the coati is active during daylight and prefers to roam in open woodlands in search of fruit, nuts, birds' eggs, lizards, and scorpions. In addition to the coati, some scientists include ringtails *(Bassariscus astutus)* in the raccoon family. These nocturnal mammals have a larger range than the coati, inhabiting Mexico and the western United States as far north as southwestern Oregon and as far east as Texas. They prefer chaparrals, rocky ridges, and cliffs not far from water. Another relative of the raccoon is the lesser panda *(Ailurus fulgens).* These animals live in the Himalayas and are not related to the bamboo-eating black-and-white pandas you may have seen in a zoo.

Raccoons are more widely distributed than any of their relatives and can be found throughout the United States, southern Canada, Mexico, and Panama. Raccoons prefer to live in and around wetlands such as marshes, swamps, and streams, but these highly adaptable creatures also thrive in cities and in suburbs where their natural habitats have been destroyed. You may have had experience with these backyard mammals of the night.

A raccoon's coat is made up of two different kinds of hair—short, fine hairs that form a dense undercover (90 percent) and longer, coarser guard hairs that give the raccoon its color (10 percent). If you've ever examined raccoon fur, you know that it is composed of a variety of colors that include shades of black, brown, gray, red, and even a touch of yellow. The fur is also streaked with white. The color and shade of this pelage vary considerably with individual raccoons and geographic location. For example, raccoons living in the Pacific Northwest have dark fur, while those living in southern regions wear a lighter-colored coat. Scientists think this variation occurs because light colors tend to reflect heat better than darker colors. We utilize this principle when we wear light colors in the summer and darker colors in the colder months of winter.

On rare occasions a white raccoon appears in the forest. Such animals generally have faint yellow markings that substitute for the black face mask and tail rings. Pure albino raccoons, those with white fur and pink eyes, are extremely rare. Perhaps most unusual are raccoons that are completely black.

Raccoons shed their coats each year, beginning in March. Hair loss

lesser, or red, panda
(Ailurus fulgens)

coati
(Nasua narica)

ringtail
(Bassariscus astutus)

not to scale

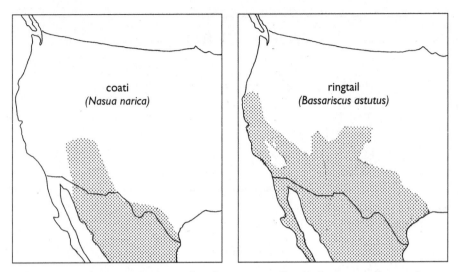

The coati is active during the day and prefers open woodlands; the nocturnal ringtail prefers chaparrals, rocky ridges, and cliffs.

begins at the head and progresses systematically to the tip of the tail. If you see a raccoon in April that looks a big ragged, you can reasonably assume it's shedding—raccoons often lose large patches of hair at one time.

Since raccoons are nocturnal, we generally don't see those that live in the forests unless we find a den in a tree hollow. But if you are alert and learn their telltale signs, you can learn a great deal about these shy animals. For example, although their dens are extremely clean, raccoons are not so fussy about the appearance of the grounds below. Raccoons don't mind leaving their scat (dried feces) scattered around the base of the trees. They also leave these "calling cards" along the branches they rest on during the day. Dens are frequently found in the hollows of hardwood trees such as basswood, maple, sycamore, beech, oak, and sweet gum, but since raccoons are very adaptable, you can also find them living comfortably in abandoned wood duck boxes, empty woodchuck burrows, sewer conduits, and church steeples. They will even share lodging with other living things in barns, garages, sheds, and houses.

We know that raccoons are clever animals. Their lumbering, bearlike gait belies the shrewd animal that thrives on its wit. When we find raccoons sharing space with us, we usually object. We forget that it is our need for housing, roads, and shopping malls that has destroyed the natural habitats of these small mammals and they are simply putting their adaptive strategies to work.

THE WORLD OF RACCOONS

What to Bring	Science Skills
basic kit	*observing*
camera	*recording*
binoculars	*inferring*
a sense of humor	

OBSERVATIONS

These smart nocturnal mammals prefer to live in marshy places and wooded areas that border the banks of streams and rivers. They also find a suitable life on rocky cliffs where a water supply is not far away. Man has destroyed much of these natural habitats, but raccoons are highly adaptable. You can expect to find them in increasing numbers on farmlands, in urban parks, and in suburban backyards—anywhere they can find adequate food and water and acceptable den sites. In their search for these necessities, raccoons have inhabited church steeples, sewers, sheds, and even parking garages.

When to Look for Them. During the late summer and autumn, raccoons spend a lot of time foraging for food so that they can accumulate a hefty layer of fat that will sustain them through the winter. Raccoons are especially active

common nighthawk
(*Chordeiles minor*)

whippoorwill
(*Caprimulgus vociferus*)

If you see nightjars seining insects from the air, you can expect to see a foraging raccoon in the area.

Raccoons make repeated daytime use of hollow trees that will become their winter dens.

during warm, moist nights because these conditions cause odors to be more pronounced. This makes it easier for raccoons to pick up the scent of food. Do you find that smells are more noticeable under similar conditions? If goatsuckers (nightjars) such as the common nighthawk *(Chordeiles minor)*, whippoorwill *(Caprimulgus vociferus)*, chuck-will's-widow *(Caprimulgus carolinensis)* and poor-will *(Phalaenoptilus nuttallii)* are seining insects from the air, you can expect to see a foraging raccoon in the area. Common nighthawks will not fly if there is a great horned owl in the vicinity, however, and since raccoons are also among the favorite foods of these large predatory birds, they also play it safe.

The Den. *Den* is the name given to that place where a raccoon will spend the winter. Although raccoons most often choose tree hollows as den sites, they also may overwinter in caves or rock crevices, inside rotting logs, beneath clumps of dried marsh grass, or in cavities beneath tree roots. When looking for tree dens, remember that tree holes do not have to be large; even large raccoons can fit through a hole that has a diameter of only three and one-half inches. Look for scat on the ground around the tree and for grizzled brown fur

raccoon
(Procyon lotor)

on the tree bark. If there is a cover of snow on the ground, raccoon footprints are another clue you can use.

Sometimes a raccoon will creep into a woodchuck burrow. This is particularly convenient because, as a true hibernator, the woodchuck has retired into a side chamber and is in such a deep sleep that the raccoon's presence goes unnoticed.

Resting Places. A raccoon may choose a different spot each day for sunning itself or sleeping. Daytime resting sites may be in buildings, in wooded areas, or in wetlands such as swamps or salt marshes. Because they enjoy sunning themselves, look for them on rock ledges or along the banks of streams and ponds. Tree limbs or even abandoned squirrel nests are also highly desirable resting places. If you find a raccoon curled up on the branch of a tree, you will discover what good camouflage the ringed tail offers the critter as it naps. An urban cousin is likely to pass the day in an abandoned building, a chimney, or some other comfortable man-made structure.

Raccoons are known to leave a resting place to forage shortly after sunset and return to it or a different place an hour or so before sunrise. Look for resting places in your area. How long after sunset does the raccoon leave the resting place? Though it frequently selects a different spot each day, a raccoon may choose the same daytime resting place. Does the raccoon leave this place at the same time each evening, or is it somewhat flexible?

Close-up of a Raccoon. When you find a raccoon, take some time to observe it. A pair of binoculars is helpful, especially if the raccoon is some distance away from you. Another possibility is to observe a roadkill, but avoid touching the animal and be careful of traffic.

Does the raccoon have a stocky build, or is its body streamlined like a squirrel? Is its nose pointed? Describe its ears. Can the raccoon turn them in the direction of a sound? What color are its eyes? How many rings are on its tail? How long is it? Is the tail longer or shorter than the raccoon's body? (See Chapter Note 1.)

Make a sketch of the raccoon and color it with crayons or paint. You may prefer to use a camera to document your observations. A zoom lens would be helpful. Add these pictures to your notebook.

Gait. If you get a chance to observe a live raccoon, describe the way it moves. Does it move slowly? Does it carry its head straight ahead, or does the head move from side to side? Does it walk like a dog? Describe the gait when a raccoon is frightened or in a hurry. Compare this with the gait the raccoon uses when foraging. (See Chapter Note 2.)

Footprints. Raccoons forage along streams and muddy riverbanks during the summer and fall. You can expect to find them out of their dens during warm spells throughout the winter. If a watercourse is affected by tides, the best time to look for footprints is at low tide. Your local newspaper will provide tidal information for your area.

Raccoon tracks are easy to identify because the animals walk on the soles of their feet with the heels touching the ground, much like bears and humans. Raccoon prints look a lot like those of a small child.

When you find some footprints, try to tell a story about the foraging ani-

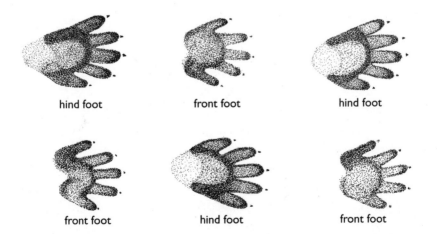

hind foot	front foot	hind foot
front foot	hind foot	front foot

The lumbering walk of a raccoon is unique: No other animal leaves tracks with this two-by-two pattern. The front and hind feet alternate sides in each group of two tracks.

mals. How many raccoons were there? Did any of them come nose to nose with each other?

Raccoons are moderately social but usually forage alone except for females feeding with their kits. When adults meet there is a "greeting" and sometimes a playful tussle. Is there any evidence of this behavior? Were some of the raccoons heavier than others? Were they all adults or were there some kits in the group? Whenever you make inferences, be sure they can be backed up with evidence. (See Chapter Note 3.)

Eye Shine. Raccoons have binocular vision. Their eyes are equipped with a reflective membrane called the *tapetum lucidum,* which lets them make the most use of available light. The trade-off for this ability to see in dim light is that images are less clear. Often you will see their eyes glowing red in the beam of car headlights or a flashlight. This is called *eye shine* and is the result of the light reflecting off the tapetum lucidum.

Varies Voices. Raccoons are vocal creatures, as their human neighbors can verify. Anyone who lives within the range of some raccoons has heard the variety of sounds that these animals can make. When loud snarls and growls tear through the silence of the night, we usually think the neighborhood dogs are doing battle with one another. If you follow the noise to the source, you will discover that the noise comes from quarreling raccoons and not the local dogs. When angry or frightened, a raccoon can also hiss like a goose. Describe the sounds. How do they change during the battle?

Compare these noises with the sounds uttered by a mother raccoon as she forages with her young. What is the sound of frightened kits? (See Chapter Note 4.)

Body Language. Look for the following expressions as you observe raccoons at work and at play: *general annoyance*—tail lashing and whipping violently; *threat*—baring of teeth and laying back of ears, raising shoulder hackles, arching the back, and raising the tail; and *submission*—lowering the entire body to the ground and backing away from the aggressor.

Dog Fight. Raccoons and the neighborhood dogs are notorious enemies. It is not unusual for homeowners to be awakened in the wee hours of the morning to the sounds of these two animals squabbling. When matched with a dog of similar size and weight, the raccoon always seems to have the competitive edge. Its compact size, short neck, and dense fur protects its delicate skin and contributes to the raccoon's success.

Dogs will sometimes foolishly chase raccoons into a stream or pond. When the dog follows the raccoon into the water, the agile raccoon can quickly end the confrontation by pushing the dog's head underwater.

general annoyance

threat

submission

Raccoons express themselves through distinctive body language.

Despite their size, raccoons are good tree climbers.

Tree Climbing. Raccoons climb tree trunks to reach their dens, to find a resting spot, and to escape danger. Observe a raccoon climbing a tree. If it is not in a hurry, how does the raccoon move its feet? If the raccoon is being chased, it will leap up the tree. Describe the way it moves its feet. (See Chapter Note 5.)

Raccoons can descend a tree headfirst. Like other animals that climb down trees, raccoons turn their hind feet outward so that their claws can grasp the trunk more easily. For comparison observe a squirrel as it races down a tree trunk.

Raccoons also can back down a tree. When they do this you will see them use their feet alternately as they do when making a leisurely ascent.

Preferred Foods. Even though raccoons are carnivores, they have a varied diet. Examination of the stomach contents of dead raccoons reveals that 75 percent of the raccoon diet is made up of plant material, whereas only 25 percent of the diet is food from animals. Homeowners will testify that these opportunistic mammals will eat almost anything in the garbage pail, but they are becoming especially fond of the remains of ice cream, cakes, pies, and other junk food.

By observing their foraging activities in the spring, summer, and fall you can identify some of the foods raccoons will eat in the wild. The chart on the next page identifies some food preferences according to season. (See Chapter Note 6.)

When wild grapes grow purple and sweet, raccoons have a feast.

FAVORITE FOODS

Spring	Summer	Autumn	Winter[4]
insects	berries	acorns[3]	acorns
grasses	vegetables	corn	corn
corn[1]	nuts	crickets	persimmons
earthworms	wild strawberries	grasshoppers	pokeweed
crayfish[2]	raspberries	honey	hazelnuts
	blackberries	grains	cherries
	pokeberries	assorted berries	
	blueberries	nuts	

[1]Although the hungry raccoon can usually find some overlooked kernels when foraging in the cornfields, plant material is not readily available in the early spring.

[2]Crayfish make up the bulk of the raccoon diet in the early spring. With its nimble fingers, a raccoon can pluck these delectables from their hiding places under rocks in streams. The strong exoskeleton of the crayfish is no match for the sharp teeth of the raccoon.

[3]Acorns from white oaks are preferred by raccoons because of their sweet taste. Acorns from other types of oak trees are bitter because they contain a large amount of a strong-tasting substance called *tannin*.

[4]Throughout the winter, raccoons will eat whatever plant material is available. This varies depending on geographic location and the severity of the winter.

Raccoons also dine on baby rabbits, deer mice, meadow voles, squirrels, and ground-nesting birds such as quail and ring-necked pheasants. The eggs of these birds are preferred fare as well. Mud turtles, eastern painted turtles, musk turtles, and yellow-bellied turtles also make fine raccoon meals. Turtles are especially vulnerable to the skilled hands of raccoons when drought exposes them.

Predators. Raccoons are fairly large animals and good climbers, so they often successfully escape from their predators. Among the animals that seek to make a meal of the raccoon are red foxes, coyotes, wolves, great horned owls, bobcats, fishers, and man. Another survival factor is their feisty spirit. A cornered raccoon can put up a fierce battle. Outline a few raccoon food chains. Link the chains so that you have a food web.

How Does a Raccoon Eat? Observe a raccoon feeding and record what you see. A pair of binoculars may help. Does the raccoon smell the food before eating it? Does it manipulate the food with its sensitive fingers? If you are watching the raccoon feed along a watercourse, does it dip the food into the water before eating it? (See Chapter Note 7.)

Does the raccoon look over its shoulder from time to time while it eats? Does it stop feeding and stare intently in one direction? Do you hear or see what might have interrupted the raccoon? If the raccoon left the feeding area before finishing the meal, what caused this behavior—a boat, or people walking closeby? Did the raccoon leave the food or take the food with it?

If there are many hungry raccoons in an area, you may witness a pecking order emerge as the animals feed. The biggest and strongest females and their young are the first to feed. Smaller mothers are allowed to move in next, but single raccoons are at a serious disadvantage. They must wedge themselves into the feeding area between families of raccoons. It is not unusual for fights to erupt at the banquet table.

Roadkill. Many nocturnal animals are the victims of automobile collisions. Frequently this happens because roads have been built through a normal foraging area for deer, bear, rabbits, and other animals. Highways have separated the wintering grounds of frogs and toads from their breeding ponds. There are significant increases in roadkills after housing developments and shopping malls have been built. One way for you to get an idea of the number of animals that lose their lives along the roadways is to keep a record of roadkills in your area over a period of time. The animals listed in the table represent only a few of those killed on our roads. You may find others.

What information does your tally give you about the animals that live in your area? Are more of one kind of animal killed than another? Are you finding animals among the roadkill population that you did not know lived in your area? What patterns have emerged from your survey? Is one kind of animal killed more frequently in one season than another? In one area of road than another?

What possible explanations are there for these roadkills? For example, are the deaths occurring on a new road that cuts through some established home ranges? Has there been habitat destruction around the roadway? What other explanations can you find? During what seasons are most of the animals killed? What is the relationship between the time of the year and the number of animal deaths?

VERTEBRATE ANIMALS IN ROADKILL POPULATION

Animal	Date	Number	Location

MAMMALS
  rabbit
  opossum
  raccoon
  skunk
  badger
  red fox
  deer
  porcupine			

AMPHIBIANS
  frogs
  salamanders
  toads			

REPTILES
  lizards
  turtles
  snakes			

BIRDS
  songbirds
  raptors
  waterfowl			

Territory versus Home Range. Territorial behavior is not unique to humans, who fight wars over boundary lines and to protect or seize property. In fact, this behavior is widely distributed among vertebrates (animals with backbones) and it even exists among invertebrates (animals without backbones). When discussing *territory,* scientists are referring to any area that is defended by one animal from intrusion by another.

Scientists have identified two types of territories, one for breeding and raising young and the other for food and shelter. *Home range* is a concept somewhat different from territory and refers to the area over which the animal normally travels in search of food. A territory is the area within the home range that the animal protects (see illustration). This can be as large as the entire home range or as small as just the nest.

The size of home range is directly related to the body size of the animal. A medium-sized animal like a raccoon will have a home range that is larger than a tiny deer mouse. If a home range were a perfect circle, the grizzly bear (*Ursus horribilis*) would have a home range with a diameter of nine miles, whereas a raccoon would have a home range about one mile in diameter. In contrast a male eastern cottontail (*Sylvilagus floridanus*) would have a circular home range with a diameter of only a thousand feet. Carnivores have larger home ranges than those animals that eat only plants. Home ranges may be permanent, used year-round, or vary during mating or nesting season. Do you think that humans ever demonstrate the fighting or aggressive behavior over territory that we see in other species?

Scientists use some high-tech equipment to determine the home range boundaries of nocturnal mammals, but you can get an idea of the home range of some raccoons in your area by making simple observations. Make a map similar to the one below for the animal you track.

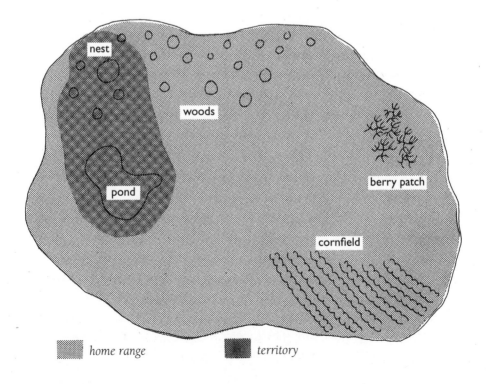

RACCOONS

CHAPTER NOTES

1. Close-up of a Raccoon. The total length of a raccoon from the tip of its nose to the tip of its tail can be from twenty-six to thirty-eight inches. Its ringed tail is generally between seven and twelve inches long and may have five to seven dark rings. This tail is used primarily for balance when the raccoon is climbing trees or walking along the branches but also serves as a muffler when sleeping in cold weather and affords camouflage to a raccoon resting in sun-dappled foliage. Male raccoons weigh between eight and twenty-five pounds, and females weigh between six and three-quarters and seventeen and one-half pounds. Raccoons weigh less in the spring and more in the fall. Raccoons that live in the Florida Keys are smaller, usually weighing a mere three to six pounds and rarely exceeding eight pounds. Raccoons in Wisconsin have been reported to weigh as much as sixty-two pounds, but some experts don't believe this figure.

2. Gait. A raccoon ambles along in a slow, lumbering way that we associate with a heavy, somewhat clumsy animal. It frequently stops to pick up an object and examine it with its dainty and sensitive fingers. You may see a raccoon stand on its hind legs. You can expect it to sit on its haunches when exploring a newfound object.

When moving faster, a raccoon trots like a dog but cannot sustain this speed for very long. When a raccoon desperately needs to escape from danger, it can bound something like a rabbit. This movement is very different than walking or trotting because each pair of feet moves together; when the front feet hit the ground, the rear feet pass outside of and forward of the front feet, and when the rear feet land, the powerful rear leg muscles launch the raccoon forward in a stretching leap so that it lands on the outstretched front feet and repeats the process. At top speed raccoons can bound along at about fifteen miles per hour, but they are unable to sustain this speed for very long because it uses a tremendous amount of energy.

3. Footprints. Raccoons' footprints reveal that their long, widely spaced toes are not webbed and their claws are not retractable like those of a cat. For a comparison, examine some cat tracks. When raccoons walk they place each hind foot on the ground so that the print shows the entire foot. In contrast a dog walks on its toes, its heels never touching the ground. (For those who like to explore unusual words, the raccoon is said to be a *plantigrade* animal, and the dog is called a *digitigrade*.)

4. Raccoon Sounds. Scientists who study animal behavior believe that vocalizations help keep family members in touch with one another. When foraging, the mother raccoon utters a soft, low-pitched purr for constant contact with her young. If she senses danger, she makes a short, explosive, yet quiet "mmm" sound to warn them. A sharp bark means fear, especially when sounded as the raccoon lowers its head. In the fall listen for the shrill, trembling screech owl–like sound as raccoons call to each other.

When hungry or frightened the young produce a high-pitched chittering. They indicate contentment by a quiet, low-pitched purr. A lost or hurt raccoon makes a pathetic cry.

5. Climbing. When leisurely climbing a tree, a raccoon will use its feet alternately; it places its right hind foot beside its left forefoot. Despite their size, raccoons make their way through the trees with the agility of squirrels. If a raccoon loses its balance it will grab onto a branch and dangle momentarily, then secure the branch with the claws of its four feet and proceed along in a slothlike fashion.

6. Food Washing. Conflicting theories have arisen about raccoons and the apparent "washing" of their food. It is believed that these animals don't dip the food in water to clean it but to get information about the food by manipulating it.

CHAPTER 12

Skunks

SILENT AND SOLITARY

Not long ago I was telling a friend some wonderful things I had discovered about the black-and-white members of the weasel family that inhabit our neighborhood. It soon became clear that my friend does not share my enthusiasm for skunks. He thinks they are aggressive, that they hunt other animals and "shoot" them with their chemical spray. He also holds other common misconceptions—that a skunk cannot release its spray if held aloft by its tail and that skunks are not seen in the winter because they hibernate. In a final display of exasperation he queried, "What good are they?"

In reality, skunks are delightful creatures, much more like Bambi's friend, Petunia, than the sneaky, aggressive animals they are reputed to be. If you spend some time observing a skunk and learning how it fits into the ecology of meadow and woodland, you will discover that this is not an animal to fear. You may even decide that it is downright likable.

Skunks are members of the weasel, or Mustelidae, family. Their relatives include such feisty animals as martens (*Martes americana*), fishers (*Martes pennanti*), weasels (*Mustela* sp.), wolverines (*Gulo luscus*), and badgers (*Taxidea taxus*), as well as minks (*Mustela vison*), river otters (*Lutra canadensis*), and sea otters (*Enhydra lutris*). One common trait shared by most members of the weasel family is their habit of foraging for food under the dark quilt of night. Most of these animals also produce strong, unpleasant odors.

Scent glands are not unique to the members of the weasel family but are present in almost all mammals, providing each species with its characteristic scent. Their function and location vary. Some mammals, like deer, have scent glands on their feet, whereas the woodchuck's are on its face. Domestic cats rub their cheeks against furniture to leave their scent on it. The black bear carries its scent glands under the skin on its back. In skunks, minks, and weasels, these glands are located in the anal region, whereas rabbits, foxes, wolves, and dogs wear theirs at the base of the tail. Although the secretions produced by the scent glands smell foul to us, they help the animals discern valuable information about visitors to their neighborhoods. Scent marks or trails can reveal the sex, size, age, and reproductive condition of an animal. They also identify the territories that belong to different males during the breeding season and send warnings to predators.

Mammals have many unusual techniques for marking scent trails. For example, bears mark trees by rubbing their backs against wet tree bark. California ground squirrels leave their marks on stones, and river otters deposit theirs on tufts of grass. Badgers are known to deposit chemical trails along the base of trees and shrubs. In the early fall I have found scent pits dug in

family Mustelidae
*Members, varied in size and color,
usually have anal scent glands.*

mink

skunk

marten

wolverine

weasel

badger

fisher

otter

the soft earth of the woodland floor by male deer. The buck deposits urine in the pit along with secretions from his scent gland, which he hopes will attract a receptive female and at the same time keep away competing males.

The odors of some mammals are stronger and more offensive than others. Musk oxen, for example, secrete strong-smelling chemicals. Wolverines emit musk when they are angry, and they also spray it on their food so that it smells "spoiled" and keeps other animals away from it. Pronghorns (*Antilocapra americana*) of the western plains and Yellowstone National Park discharge a round of musk that can be smelled up to 500 yards away to alert members of the grazing herd to danger.

All skunks are renowned for their scent glands, but those of the striped skunk are especially well developed. The skunk stores its golden-hued, foul-smelling musk in two grape-sized sacs in muscles beside its anus. A duct from each sac ends in a nipple that opens into the animal's colon, and anal muscles regulate the system. When danger threatens, the animal turns its anus inside out and exposes the nipples. The skunk can then fire its musk, but it does so only as a last resort.

Spray from a frightened skunk can travel about six feet but can hit a downwind target as far away as twenty yards. The odor from a barrage of spray can be detected for more than a half mile in all directions. Skunks can vary not only the strength of each jet but also the direction of the spray. The spray of musk fired by a skunk has been compared to a machine gun as it sweeps over a forty-five-degree angle to the right and left of center. A skunk's scent glands manufacture as little as one-third of an ounce each week, enough musk for five or six consecutive rounds. No urine is released in the process. (See Chapter Note 1.)

Skunks prefer not to spray their musk, so they depend on their reputation as their first line of defense. Even at night its bold, white-and-black fur broadcasts its presence and predators know to stay away. Some dogs ignore this warning, however, and when the night air is filled with the sulfurous smell of skunk, you can be reasonably sure a neighborhood dog encountered one.

If you come across a frightened skunk, stand still. Running away will only agitate the skunk and cause it to discharge a volley of musk. Neither of you wants this to happen. Skunks would rather ramble away from dangerous situations than spray. When skunks squabble among themselves, they never spray each other but instead scratch and bite each other with their long, curved front claws and sharp teeth. Usually neither party suffers.

Skunks have a variety of common names. The Cree Indians called it *Sikak*,

hognose skunk
(Conepatus leuconotus)

hooded skunk
(Mephitis macroura)

and the scientists who study mammals (mammalogists) call the striped skunk *Mephitis mephitis*. Derived from the Latin for "noxious vapor," the name refers to the skunk's talent for producing smelly chemicals. At one time trappers found skunk pelts could bring a handsome sum of money, so they dubbed the fur "Alaskan sable." In some rural regions of the United States, people refer to the skunk as a polecat.

While most people know a skunk when they see one, many are not aware that there are different skunk species. The most familiar is the striped skunk, which ranges across the United States into Canada and south to Central America. Another variety is the spotted skunk (*Spilogale putorius*). Although this animal is not as widely distributed as the striped skunk, the two species share similar habitats. An immigrant from South America, the hognose skunk (*Conepatus leuconotus*) lives in the American Southwest and Mexico, as does the hooded skunk (*Mephitis macroura*). Animals in other parts of the world are also called skunks, but the name technically belongs only to the New World creatures and their very close relatives.

Skunks thrive in rolling fields, fencerows, wooded ravines, rocky outcrops, and patches of brush near water. You are as apt to find them living under your front porch as in natural cavities such as caves, under felled logs, or in tree stumps. Dens abandoned by woodchucks, badgers, red foxes, and muskrats also make fine skunk housing. Sometimes they dig their own burrows, typically about three feet deep and five feet long, with one to three chambers at the end of a long entrance tunnel. Each chamber is lined with leaves, grasses, and hay. These dens sometimes have more than one entrance; when the weather turns cold, the skunks plug the entrances and remain inside until a warm spell lures them out. Although they prefer to be alone, skunks den with other skunks for the winter and sometimes even share a burrow with opossums, woodchucks, raccoons, and cottontail rabbits—although each different kind of animal has its own chamber.

Skunks do not hibernate, although they remain inactive for much of the winter in the northern part of their range, with their level of activity determined by such factors as temperature, hunger, and amount of snow cover. Skunks that live in the South forage throughout the winter.

Striped skunks are polygamous, which means they have more than one mate. Throughout much of their range, the males begin to prowl their neighborhoods in February and March, searching for females. After mating and a gestation period of sixty-two to sixty-six days, six to eight pups the size of meadow mice are born. At birth the skunks are wrinkled, thinly furred, and blind, but their pink skin already exhibits the characteristic black-and-white pattern of an adult skunk. Skunk pups are helpless, and their babyhood continues for about two months. They are unable to breed until the next spring (in contrast with the meadow mouse, which breeds one month after birth!). During their first season, you may see young skunks playing follow-the-leader with their mother at the head of the line. Striped skunks live for about two and one-half to three years in the wild and as long as ten years in captivity.

Skunks are classified as omnivores because they eat a variety of foods, but about 70 percent of their diet consists of animal matter during spring and summer, when insects are plentiful. They gobble up grasshoppers, crickets, beetles, bees, and wasps, as well as spiders, earthworms, snails, clams, crayfish, salamanders, lizards, toads, frogs, snakes, minnows, and turtle eggs.

Young skunks trail behind their mother as she teaches them how to look for good things to eat.

A hungry skunk will not pass up field mice, jumping mice, house mice, voles, rats, bats, moles, shrews, ground squirrels, chipmunks, and squirrels. Although they cannot chase speedy prey, their stealthy, catlike hunting strategies usually win them dinner. You may observe a skunk as it crouches and waits, or slowly stalks its supper. When the time is right, the skunk will pounce and trap the prey beneath its front feet.

Skunks also use their front claws to tear rotting logs and eat the insect larvae that live there. They eat twice their weight several times a week, doing away with huge quantities of agricultural pests such as cutworms, tobacco bud worms, Colorado potato beetles, hop grubs, and squash bugs. Therefore, heavy use of insecticides often inadvertently kills some insect-eating mammals such as skunks. To counter this, some years ago the skunk was recognized as an ally in the farmers' struggle against the hop beetle in New York and the state passed legislation protecting skunks.

Blackberries, black cherries, blueberries, gooseberries, persimmons, grasses, and nuts are also part of the skunk's diet in fall and winter. This ability to forage for a variety of foods is among the adaptations that have made it possible for these little mammals to survive despite the changing environment.

Before they were recognized as a four-legged insecticide, skunks were much more valued for their pelts. The more black a pelt contained, the greater price it would bring—unscrupulous furriers would sometimes sell skunk pelts to unwary or less affluent customers as mink.

Today there are practical uses for skunk musk. For instance, people who explore underground caves use it to discover connections between passageways in the caves. It has also been used effectively to curtail theft in tree farms by spraying the trees most likely to be pilfered. (Who wants a Christmas tree that reeks of skunk musk?) The odor is gone by spring, when people want to buy the trees to landscape their property.

We know that the striped skunk has contributed significantly to our welfare, but you may not know about the contributions of the spotted skunk. These animals are able to delay the implantation in the uterus of a fertilized egg, which remains suspended in very early stages of cell division. Scientists are examining this delay to discover natural methods of limiting cell division. This could help in controlling cancer, which is a problem of rapid cell division.

Even though you still may not invite a skunk for dinner, a little respect is called for. After all, the great city of Chicago (Sikako) was named in its honor. Let's hear it for the skunk.

THE WORLD OF SKUNKS

What to Bring
basic kit
camera with telephoto lens
binoculars
determination

Science Skills
observing
recording

OBSERVATIONS

Striped Skunk *(Mephitis mephitis).* Although skunks are considered nocturnal animals, they often begin foraging during the late afternoon or early evening hours. They have a fine sense of smell and very good hearing, important since they hunt at night. Striped skunks are nearsighted, however, which makes it relatively easy for us to get close to them. If you move quietly and slowly toward a grazing skunk, you can usually get within ten feet of it without disturbing it. If this makes you nervous, you can make accurate observations from as far away as twenty feet. The skunk will use its warning system to tell you if you get too close. Remember, the skunk does not want to spray you, so back away when you see it raise its tail.

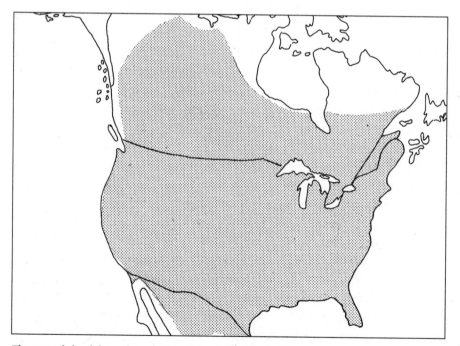

The striped skunk has a broad range throughout North America.

Close-up of a Striped Skunk. If there is sufficient light when you find your skunk, take a picture of it. A telephoto lens will help you focus on details that are easily overlooked. How big is the skunk? Describe its body, ears, and eyes. Photographs are effective methods for recording your observations, but you should also keep written records because shadows and dim lighting can cause a photo to look somewhat different than the subject.

Color Variations. Striped skunks are not carbon copies of each other. As you begin to observe them, look for variations in the patterns of their fur. Describe the black-and-white pattern on the fur and draw a picture of it. As you practice observing striped skunks, you will notice individual pattern differences that will help you distinguish one skunk from another. (See Chapter Note 2.)

Daytime Skunks. Although skunks are generally nocturnal, you may find one foraging during the day, especially during warm winter days. You also can expect to see newly weaned skunks foraging in cornfields, hay fields, pastures, fencerows, and along waterways in daylight. Although nocturnal animals that have the disease rabies are often seen out of their dens during the day, they usually exhibit more than one behavioral abnormality such as aggression toward other animals. If unusual behavior raises questions about the health of a particular skunk, call a wildlife specialist. Do not harm the skunk or approach it.

Gait and Speed. How do the front legs and hind legs differ from each other? Are they the same length? Describe the way the skunk walks. What is the effect of the design of their legs on their gait? Do you think a skunk could climb the chain-link fence that surrounds many chicken houses? Explain your answer. How fast can it move? (See Chapter Note 3.) Compare the speed of a striped skunk with that of other nocturnal mammals such as raccoons, opossums, and cottontail rabbits.

Voice. Skunks are quiet animals. They hunt and play in silence, although when a fight breaks out between two skunks you will hear a barrage of growls, squeals, and hisses. When foraging or when tending their pups, you may hear soft grunts, growls, barks, and churrings. Snarls and twitters that resemble those made by birds and squirrels are also in the skunk vocabulary. Describe the sounds you hear. What was the skunk doing when it made the sounds?

The Warning. It is well known that skunks will not discharge a blast of musk without ample warning, so it is a good idea to learn how to recognize it. An unconcerned, relaxed striped skunk ambles along with its tail nearly touching the ground. As the first signal in the warning system the skunk may stamp its front feet. It does this rapidly and loudly enough that you can hear

The striped skunk (Mephitis mephitis) *assumes its infamous* U *posture before spraying musk.*

it several yards away. You may also hear growls or hissing sounds at this time. Many skunks omit this first step and proceed directly to the tail-raising signal. In this stage the major portion of the tail is held erect, but the tip may flop over to one side. The long guard hairs along the entire length of the tail stick out at right angles to it. This makes the tail look extremely large. Immediately before musking, the skunk assumes its infamous U posture, at which time its head and tail directly face the intruder. If you are still considered a threat at this point, the skunk will probably spray you. (See Chapter Note 4.)

Myths. Like other creatures of the night, many myths surround the lives and habits of skunks. Following is a list of some of them:

• *Musk can damage your eyes.* The truth is that although musk can cause intense burning, it does not cause permanent damage to the eyes.

• *Skunks spray musk with their tails.* Scientists know that they spray with nipples that are connected to anal sacs.

• *Musk is made of urine.* Musk has its own chemical composition that is very different from skunk urine.

• *Skunks are aggressive.* They are not. They are among the peaceable animals in the forest.

EXPLORATIONS

Roadkill. One way to determine whether there are skunks in your neighborhood is to make a systematic survey of the roadkill population. You will want to make your survey over a period of time, say for about one year. During what season do you find the most roadkilled skunks? Why do you think this is so? What habitats are in the vicinity of the roadkills—farmland, meadows, wooded areas, fields? Is it a suburban community or a city? In addition to skunks, what other animals are among the roadkills?

Dental Formula. The dental formula for the striped skunk is as follows:

$$I \frac{3}{3}, C \frac{1}{1}, P \frac{3}{3}, M \frac{1}{2} = 34$$

How does this compare with the dental formulas of the raccoon and the opossum? How do the dental formulas of these animals compare with your dental formula? How can you explain the differences in formulas between these animals and human beings? See chapter 9 for an explanation of the dental formula.

Home Range. Home ranges for male skunks are usually larger than they are for females. Male striped skunks have home ranges with a diameter of 1 to 1½ miles Females meander within a range of 600 to 700 feet in diameter. Do you think that roadkills are more likely to be males or females? Find a den occupied by a striped skunk. Figure out what the boundaries of the home range might be and draw a map of it. If you work on this activity and the one below that deals with food chains with a friend, you will add to your fun.

Food Chain/Web. The introduction to this chapter should give you a good idea of what foods skunks prefer and what foods they will eat if the preferred foods are not available. Make a survey of your community to find out what skunk foods are present. A food web that includes other animals such as raccoons, opossums, and owls and that shows interrelationships between these animals would be fun and informative to construct. Will these animals be well fed if they forage in your community?

Skunk Signs. There are a few signs that will help you determine if there are skunks in your neighborhood:

• Their distinctive odor.

• Pits dug in the ground or lawn that are one to two inches deep and three to four inches across, where a skunk has been digging for insects.

• Tracks in soft mud or in damp sandy soils (in a running gait, generally less than one foot apart).

• Scats.

Skunk at the Roadside. Many people believe that skunks get killed along the road because they "stand their ground" and don't have the sense to flee from oncoming cars. If you have ever seen a skunk in the beam of your headlights, you know that its first response is to flee. Unfortunately, automobiles are faster than skunks. If any predator continues to follow a skunk, it then issues its sequence of warning signals. Of course, none of them work with a car. The only defense left to the skunk is its infamous spray, which has no effect on the automobile. The skunk becomes another roadside casualty. The next time you see a skunk approached by a car, observe the skunk's behavior.

Predators. Skunks have few predators, including bobcats, great horned owls, domestic dogs, and foxes, but skunks are reasonably safe from even these skilled predators because they seek skunks only if pressed to do so by extreme hunger. Are any of these predators living near you? Look for evidence of them such as owl pellets, scat, and footprints.

Scent Trail. It's not enough just to leave a scent trail. Mammals are continuously reading the messages left by other animals, especially those of the same species. You may not have an opportunity to follow an animal in the wild as it reads one of these trails, but if you would like to find out how this

The walking pattern of the striped skunk is irregular but shows the hind feet overstepping the front.

Striped skunk scat is usually black and much bigger than you might think. It may reach three-quarters of an inch or more in diameter.

works, call your local branch of the American Kennel Club. They can tell you how dogs are trained to track a scent. You may even have an opportunity to see how it's done.

OTHER SKUNKS

Spotted Skunk *(Spilogale putorius).* This little skunk is smaller than its cousin the striped skunk. Its weight ranges from a mere three-fourths of a pound to two and three-fourths pounds, and its total length can be from about fourteen inches to twenty-two inches. Generally, the spotted skunk

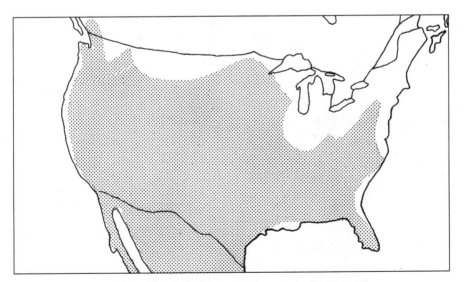

The spotted skunk is found from coast to coast in the United States.

doesn't venture from its den until after nightfall, and it is more secretive than the striped skunk.

The spotted skunk can travel at a rate of about four miles per hour. They are good tree climbers, but they prefer to remain on the ground except when being chased by dogs.

Their diet is similar to that of the striped skunk. They are omnivores that prefer animal food, especially in the summer when grasshoppers, crickets, and beetles are available. Mice are another important food item, especially during winter. Rats, small mammals, rabbits, birds' eggs, disabled birds, lizards, snakes, salamanders, crayfish, and mushrooms are eaten when available. Spotted skunks, like their relatives, are valuable members of the farm community.

They are preyed on by dogs, domestic cats, great horned owls, bobcats, and human beings.

Alarm Display. The spotted skunk has a fascinating alarm display. Like the striped skunk, its gives its first warning by stamping its feet and then raising its tail. If these signs do not deter the intruder, the spotted skunk displays its famous handstand. When raised up on its two front feet it looks larger than it really is, and its agility in this position rivals that of a high-wire performer. There is no doubt that the spotted skunk can spray in this position; it does not have to have four feet on the ground in order to do so.

The spotted skunk performs its famous handstand before musking.

Hooded Skunk *(Mephitis macroura)*. These skunks live very close to the Mexican border and come in two varieties; one has a nearly all-white back, and the back of the other is essentially black.

Hognose Skunk *(Conepatus leuconotus)*. This skunk with the piglike snout also prefers the Southwest and Mexico. Its all-white back and black underparts testify to its membership in the skunk clan.

Further Research Is Needed. Scientists are exploring many areas of skunk life. Some of these are related to the denning habits of skunks, their reproductive biology, and their distribution in a local area or throughout a wider range. If you are interested in getting involved in a skunk project, call your local nature center or the extension service of a state university. They may be able to steer you in the right direction.

CHAPTER NOTES

1. Folklore. It is a commonly held belief that a skunk cannot fire its musk when it is held up by its tail. That statement is true as long as you grab the skunk by its tail *before* it exposes the nipples of the scent ducts (those tubes that lead from the scent sacs to the nipples). If you grab the skunk by the tail *after* this happens, you will surely get sprayed. In order to know if the nipples are exposed, you would have to get closer to the skunk than would be prudent.

2. Description of Striped Skunk. From the tip of the nose to the tip of its tail, a mature skunk measures about twenty to thirty inches and weighs about three and one-half to ten pounds. Their size is generally compared to that of a full-grown house cat. The males are usually heavier than the females, and the largest males are found in Wisconsin. Skunks have small, black eyes that some have described as "beady." They generally have poor eyesight—it is not unusual for two skunks to pass each other on a path without realizing the other was there. Their ears are rounded and short and resemble those of a raccoon. Their shiny black appearance is due to long, glossy guard hairs that overlay soft underfur.

The fur of the striped skunk is normally black and white, but seal-brown and cream colored fur occur rarely. Albino skunks, with all-white fur and pink eyes, are also seen occasionally.

3. Speed and Legs. As you might have guessed from the design of the legs, striped skunks are not agile and they do not climb well. They have been clocked ambling along at 1.6 miles per hour. They can run over the ground at about 3 or 4 miles per hour, with a top speed of 6 mph. This relatively slow speed makes them easy prey for dogs. Although skunks usually avoid

water, they have been known to remain in cold water (23 degrees C) for seven hours to escape dogs. The toes on each foot are slightly webbed, which probably helps when the skunk swims.

When skunks walk, they put the entire sole of the foot on the ground like we do. Animals that walk in this way are said to be *plantigrade*. Look for prints of the five long, down-curved claws on the front feet. The claws on the hind feet are shorter and straighter, and these claws rarely show in a footprint.

4. Antidote for Musk. There are as many antidotes for removing skunk musk as there are people who have been sprayed by it. One large can of tomato juice, perhaps two, is usually sufficient to neutralize the musk sprayed on one small boy and a dog.

Although it may seem inconceivable for those who find the smell of skunk musk offensive, there are those who find the odor quite pleasant, at least in small doses. The tolerance for this odor appears to be genetic.

SELECTED BIBLIOGRAPHY

THE STAGE

Ackerman, Diane. *Natural History of the Senses*. New York: Random House, 1990.

Evans, William F. *Communication in the Animal World*. New York: Thomas Y. Crowell, 1968.

Kappel-Smith, Diane. *Night Life: Nature from Dusk to Dawn*. Boston: Little, Brown, and Company, 1990.

SMELL

Comfort, A. "Communication May be Odorous." *New Scientist* 49 (February 25, 1971): 412–414.

Ferrara, J. L. "Why Vultures Make Good Neighbors." *National Wildlife* (June–July 1987): 16–20.

Gilbert, A. N., and C. J. Wysocki. "The Smell Survey: Its results." *National Geographic* 172 (October 1987): 514–525.

Loewer, Peter. *The Evening Garden*. New York: Macmillan Publishing Company, 1993.

Silverstein, Alvin, et al. *Smell, the Subtle Sense*. New York: Morrow Junior Books, 1992.

Weintraub, P. "Scentimental Journeys." *Omni* (April 1986): 48–52; 114–116.

Woodworth, Robert S., and Harold Schlosberg. *Experimental Psychology*. New York: Holt, Rinehart, and Winston, 1954.

SOUND
Stevens, S. S., and Fred Warshofsky. *Sound and Hearing*. New York: Time-Life Books, 1970.

OWLS
Alcorn, Gordon Dee. *Owls: An Introduction for the Amateur Naturalist*. New York: Prentice-Hall Press, 1986.

Johnsgard, Paul A. *North American Owls: Biology and Natural History*. Washington, DC: Smithsonian Institution Press, 1988.

Maslow, Jonathan Evan. *The Owl Papers*. New York: Vintage Books, 1988.

Payne, R. S. "How the Barn Owl Locates Prey by Hearing," *The Living Bird* 1 (1962): 151–89.

Stokes, Donald, and Lillian Stokes. *A Guide to Bird Behavior,* Vol. 111. Boston: Little, Brown and Company, 1989.

FROGS
Ashton, Ray E., and Patricia Sawyer Ashton. *The Amphibians*. Miami: Windward Publishing Inc., 1988.

Smith, Hobart M. *A Guide to Field Identification: Amphibians of North America*. New York: Golden Press, 1978.

Stebbins, R. C. *A Field Guide to Western Reptiles and Amphibians*. Boston: Houghton Mifflin Company, 1966.

Tyning, Thomas. *A Guide to Amphibians and Reptiles*. Boston: Little, Brown and Company, 1990.

MOTHS
Covell, Charles V. *A Field Guide to the Moths of Eastern North America*. Boston: Houghton Mifflin Company, 1984.

Holland, W. J. *The Moth Book: A Guide to the Moths of North America*. New York: Dover, 1968.

Mitchell, Robert T., and Herbert Zim. *Butterflies and Moths: A Guide to the More Common Species*. New York: Golden Press, 1964.

Wright, Amy Bartlett. *Caterpillars: A Simplified Field Guide to the Caterpillars of Common Butterflies and Moths of North America*. Boston: Houghton Mifflin Company, 1993.

FIREFLIES

Harrison, George. "Fireflies: Lights of Love." *Sports Afield* (July 1982): 32–33.

Peterson, Ivars. "Step in Time." *Science News* 140: 136–137.

White, Richard E. *Beetles: A Field Guide to the Beetles of North America*. Boston: Houghton Mifflin Company, 1983.

BATS

Gibbons, Ann. "Is 'Flying Primate' Hypothesis Headed for a Crash Landing?" *Science* (April 3, 1992): 34.

Goodman, Billy. "Holy Phylogeny! Did Bats Evolve Twice?" *Science* (July 5, 1991): 36.

Halton, Cheryl Mays. *Those Amazing Bats*. Minneapolis: Dillon Press Inc., 1992.

Pringle, L. *Batman: Exploring the World of Bats*. New York: Charles Scribner's Sons, 1991.

Tuttle, Merlin D. *America's Neighborhood Bats*. Austin: University of Texas Press, 1988.

Yalden, D. W., and P. A. Morris. *The Lives of Bats*. New York: Quadrangle Press, The New York Times Book Company, 1975.

HOPPERS

Dethier, Vincent G. *Crickets and Katydids: Concerts and Solos*. Cambridge, MA: Harvard University Press, 1992.

Sakaluk, Scott K. "Sex for a Song (Dinner Included)." *Natural History* (September 1991): 67–72.

White, Richard E. *Beetles: A Field Guide to the Beetles of North America*. Boston: Houghton Mifflin Company, 1983.

RACCOONS, OPOSSUMS, AND SKUNKS

Burt, William H., and Richard P. Grossenheider. *A Field Guide to the Mammals*, 3rd ed. Boston: Houghton Mifflin Company, 1976.

Chapman, Joseph A., and George A. Feldhamer, eds. *Wild Mammals of North America*. Baltimore: Johns Hopkins University Press, 1982.

Hall, E. Raymond, and Keith A. Kelson. *The Mammals of North America*. New York: John Wiley and Sons Inc. 1989.

Nowak, Ronald. *Walker's Mammals of the World*, 5th ed. Baltimore: The Johns Hopkins University Press, 1991.

TAPES AND RECORDINGS

A Field Guide to Bird Songs of Eastern and Central North America. Ithaca, NY: Cornell Laboratory of Ornithology, 1983. (607) 254-2404.

Voices of the Night: The Calls of the Frogs and Toads of Eastern North America. Ithaca, NY: Cornell Laboratory of Ornithology. (607) 254-2404.